The Boxer

Kay White

John Bartholomew & Son Limited
Edinburgh

The Publisher wishes to thank The Kennel Club and The American Kennel Club for permission to reproduce the breed standards.

First published in Great Britain 1977 *by*
JOHN BARTHOLOMEW & SON LIMITED
12 Duncan Street, Edinburgh EH9 1TA

© *John Bartholomew & Son Limited,* 1977
All rights reserved. No part of this publication may be reproduced, stored in a retrieval system, or transmitted, in any form, or by any means, electronic, mechanical, photocopying, recording, or otherwise, without the prior permission of John Bartholomew & Son Limited

ISBN 0 7028 1035 5

1st edition

Reprinted 1982, 1984, 1986, 1987

Prepared for the Publisher by Youé & Spooner Ltd.
Colour illustrations by Charles Rush; airbrush drawings by Malcolm Ward; diagrams pages 21, 22, 23, 27 by Harold White

Printed in Great Britain by John Bartholomew & Son Limited

Contents

Preface

The Boxer is a comparatively modern breed that has achieved wide popularity in a relatively short space of time. When you read this book you can well understand why. The author, who has loved and kept the breed for many years, has portrayed the Boxer with exceptional clarity and vivacity. Here is a portrait of a boisterous clown of a dog who with the right firm handling makes a sensible family companion and an exceptional guard. All aspects relating to the care and upbringing of a family pet are fully dealt with and the whole book is enlivened with vignettes of the author's own dogs. All Boxer enthusiasts will want to own this book, and many others, to whom the breed is less familiar, are likely to be converted to 'Boxermania' after reading it.

Wendy Boorer
Consultant Editor

Breed history

The Boxer was created by German breeders, as a deliberate variant on the Bullenbeisser, the bull baiting dog, or the bull dog not to be confused with the modern Bulldog, which has been drastically altered physically in the last hundred years. The active, courageous bull dog has existed all over Europe since the Middle Ages. Bull baiters were in their turn the smaller descendants of the large Mastiff type fighting dogs of Roman times.

The cult of breeding pedigree dogs goes back less than 150 years, but breeding for type and ability has been practised ever since canines were domesticated, in order to select dogs with the best qualities for the work they were intended to do. Strong dogs with powerful jaws were needed to kill boar and deer in the Middle Ages. These dogs came in at the end of the hunt when the quarry had been tracked down by lighter, fast running dogs with good scenting power, the hounds.

As well as providing food and an exciting chase, bull and bear baiting became popular spectator sports on feast and fair days in seventeenth-century Britain, offering an excitement for the villagers and an opportunity for gambling. The pastime spread quickly across Europe, in times when violence and cruelty were much more part of everyday life.

In Britain a bull would be tethered, probably on the village green, and local worthies would set their dogs upon the bull, the object being for the dog to grasp the bull by the nose, while avoiding being flung high on the bull's horns, or pounded by the hooves. Bets were placed on which dog would last the longest. Although grievous injury was often inflicted on the dogs, the bull was the inevitable loser, although sometimes it would break free and add to the excitement by rampaging through houses, causing a stampede. Meat from the baited bull was greatly prized, as it was thought to be extra tender, due to the great output of blood and adrenalin during the bull's struggles.

Inevitably the bull baiting dogs began to be kept by butchers, both as meat tenderisers and professional fighters, so the bull-type dog became known as the butcher's dog, rather despised by the nobility who kept their packs of hounds, their elegant bird-dogs, and the ladies' pets or toy dogs. It was soon evident that the dogs which excelled at bull baiting were the smaller animals which attacked low to the ground, avoiding the bull's horns. The dogs needed to be agile, strong in-forequarters and flexible behind, with powerful thigh muscles. Broad, wide-gripping jaws were essential, and a short, set back nose helped the dog to breathe while holding its quarry. In character, the bull baiter needed great courage, to the point of foolhardy steadfastness against its huge adversary, and also a certain insensitivity to the pain of wounds inflicted during the fight.

The life of the Bullenbeisser in sixteenth-century Germany was rather different; they were kept in packs at the great houses of the German nobility, and used for hunting oxen, boars and bears when these animals ranged wild in the great European forests. Bullenbeisser often wore protective clothing, probably of padded sacking, quilted to save the dog from the boar's tusks.

They were certainly very fierce, and yet we are told that their quality of devotion to humans showed through, so that although kept and bred in enclosed colonies, they did not become totally pack-minded, as hounds will do.

A German treatise on dogs, dated 1719, contains the following description of the bull and bear baiter: 'It is of medium size, heavily built with a powerful chest, big head, and short pushed-in muzzle. The ears are cropped, and also the tail, when young. They are kept on leashes and accustomed to hunting medium-sized boar before they are trained for hunting bears or taught bull baiting. They are also used as guard and watch dogs, their grotesque looks being enough. Most of them have short muzzles, with black masks and undershot mouths. They are yellow and brown striped, and have a fierce appearance.'

When bull baiting declined as a sport in Britain, banned by the Humane Act of 1865, the butcher's dogs still survived, as cattle drovers, guards and as protagonists in the dog fights which still went on in secret. In Europe, the Bullenbeisser was adapted to another form of work, drawing small carts, a job which the powerful shoulder muscles made quite easy. We may feel that at this time, in the one to one situation of a weekly journey to market, the Bullenbeisser became very close to its master, and laid the foundation for the strain of working dogs which would also thrive on companionship with humans.

The British had long been acknowledged as the premier breeders of domestic animals, and many of the British bull dogs were sent over to Europe, where the Germans brought to the hobby and science of dog breeding a discipline and inventiveness that is particularly their own. To the German perseverance in mixing, matching and combining in orderly fashion we owe the Schnauzer, the Dobermann, the Dachshund varieties, and also the Boxer, among other breeds.

In the German military cult which began during the mid-nineteenth century, the breeding of specialised dogs for war purposes became important, and it is said that a German officer created a new breed from a mixture of the bull and bear baiting strains, naming it the Boxtl, or Boxer.

The Bullenbeisser often wore protective clothing when boar hunting

7

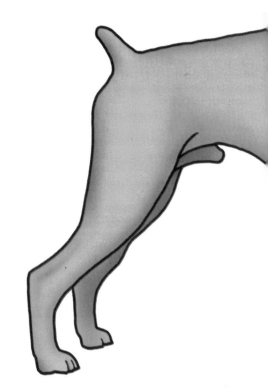

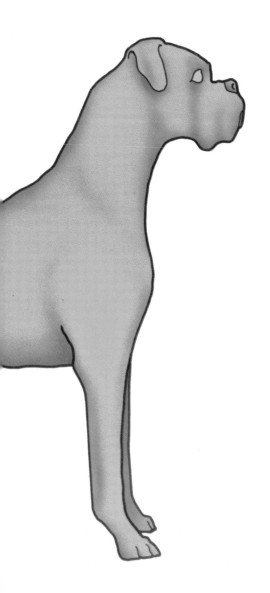

There have been many theories put forward about this very British name for a German dog, the favourite being to associate the name with the sparring use of the front paws in pugilistic fashion, the old fighting qualities being perpetuated by the name. On the other hand, 'Boxer' had been a favourite name for the working farm horse in Britain long before this time, the name probably being chosen to echo the strength and virility of the bare-fisted fighters of travelling fairs. Another theory has it that a dog named Boxl was one of the early ingredients in the new breed and yet another that Beisser (biter) may have sounded like Boxer to British ears; but we have irrefutable evidence that the name was adopted first of all in Germany, where the first Boxer to be exhibited, and to be entered in the new breed stud book as Boxer No.1, was whelped in 1895. This dog, a brindle male named Flocki, (a common dog name in Germany) was not the first Boxer of all. He was the grandson of an unnamed Boxer on his dam's side, by a bitch of unknown breeding, bought in France.

There was undoubtedly a group of enthusiasts in the Munich area working on the Boxer at this time, and Flocki must have pleased them, as he was the only dog entered at the Munich Show of that year, and was evidently approved by a large faction of the breeders, although the father of Boxer No.1 was a white British bull dog, but of a very different type from those we know today. At this time, many different breeds were being used to perfect the Boxer. Some Bull Terrier, Bull Dog, Great Dane, Giant Schnauzer, and perhaps Dalmatian blood, was incorporated.

After Flocki's debut, the German Boxer Club was founded in Munich in 1896, with an aim to bring order to the breed, but it was not until 1905 that a standard was agreed to which breeders could work. Many of the Boxers at this time were white, or white with brindle or red patches, known as 'checks', and there were also blacks, and blue blacks, due to Schnauzer blood. By 1910 the German Boxer Club had become a national body, with branches all over the country, and acknowledged officials and leaders to guide new breeders.

About this time, the greatest Boxer breeders and enthusiasts of all time, Friederun and Philip Stockmann, acquired a dog with 'a wildly happy temperament, a thick head, black face, and striped like a tiger,' the first of the famous Von Dom line to which nearly all the Boxers today can trace their ancestry, many generations back.

Frau Stockmann's book, *My Life with Boxers* will enchant everyone interested in the breed. It tells of the struggles the Stockmann family went through during two world wars and times of hunger and poverty during which they kept the strain of their Boxers going, and all the pleasure and pain that breeding dogs brings, even to us in a reasonably affluent society. Frau Stockmann was by profession an artist and sculptor, so we also owe to her the drawings and photographs of the early Boxers which illustrate her book. She tells us that the whites and checks were quickly eliminated, by never using them for breeding, or if one was used, breeding back to solid colour for several generations. Apart from other considerations, white was not an acceptable colour for a dog destined for war and police duties.

The black Boxers might have been suitable. They must have looked quite

A red Boxer on guard

terrifying, but this colour was ruled out óf the standard through personal rivalry and a concerted dislike of the man who specialised in blacks. As the standard formulated by the Munich Boxer Club became the model for others the world over, there are no black Boxers today, although the darkest brindles appear black at a distance. We still have a big percentage of white puppies born, the number increasing all the time, though the majority are destroyed at birth as few breeders are willing to rear puppies which have little monetary value and so may have a doubtful future.

The ears of the German Boxer were cropped, and the tail docked, as befitted a dog whose fighting ancestors were stripped of any unnecessary appendages. Continental and American Boxers are cropped to this day, although cropping is not allowed in Britain, and an imported dog with cropped ears may not be exhibited for competition at British Kennel Club shows. Tails are still docked all over the world, but in Norway a ban on all mutilations will come into force in 1977. Regulations in that country will then also forbid elective hysterectomy on bitches and may herald the beginning of a world revulsion against cosmetic mutilations.

The Germans were able to make rapid improvements in the breèd, because enthusiasts submitted willingly to control by breed wardens. All dogs and bitches registered in the early stud book had to be approved by the Boxer Club, and they also had to win a prize at a show. Later the breed wardens' powers were extended to approving matings, supervising the quality of pups and numbers the breeder might rear.

Strict breed control still applies in Germany today. Before any animal is bred from, it is evaluated for quality, for degree of hip dysplasia, and must also pass a low degree police test as a guarantee of true Boxer character. The dog and bitch must both show enough spirit to attack a criminal which is threatening its owner. In addition one partner of the mating, usually the male, must have passed the first grade of a more stringent police test. In this manner the true guard dog character is perpetuated, and the original purpose of this working breed is not lost.

A breed warden and vice president of the German Boxer Club in 1974, Mr Gerhard Lampe, has said in the magazine *Boxerama* that Boxer temperament is fashioned by hereditary instincts and then further influenced by environmental factors. He goes on to enumerate the factors of Boxer character: courage to stand firm against danger; guarding instinct, to act without regard to personal safety; fighting instinct, to take up the challenge to battle with enthusiasm when necessary; keenness, to persevere with their task; hardness, to remain uninfluenced by unpleasant conditions; tractability, a readiness to be guided and taught; a dog full of life, alert, displaying a keen interest in its surroundings, able to grasp ideas suggested to it quickly.

Even with breed control, the Boxer in Germany is softening up, to the regret of the hard core of breeders, but this is due, as it is in Britain and America, to the need to keep the Boxer in domestic surroundings where any sign of aggressiveness is quickly quelled. We enjoy owning a guard dog, so long as its guarding remains on the level of the threat rather than action. In practice it is difficult to test the courage and character of the Boxer, except at organised working trials. If we accept that the dog can scent fear and apprehension, then even this situation, with a stranger wearing a padded suit acting as criminal, does not present a true emergency to the dog. Many Boxers will pass their whole lives guarding their homes against callers without ever encountering someone with evil intent against their owner, so they never have the opportunity to prove their worth.

In Germany today, breed regulations are most strict. No dog with a testicular fault can be exhibited or bred from, nor can an animal with light eyes. Pedigrees are issued officially by the Munich Boxer Club, and so are more authenticated than the informal handwritten pedigree supplied by the breeder in Britain. In the UK there are no restrictions on breeding, nor on registering the progeny, of dogs with major, or minor faults; and dogs with only one testical descended into the scrotum, the unilateral crypt-orchid, (sometimes referred to as a mono-orchid) can be exhibited, and such dogs have won their way through to status as Champions.

There are very few big kennels breeding Boxers in Germany and most breeding is done by novices owning one or two bitches, so the guidance of the Boxer Club officials is welcomed. In Britain and America, with a multiplicity of medium-sized kennels, the system would not be so acceptable. Some British breeders wish that more was done to perpetuate the true 'bull dog' temperament, but since the Boxer is a popular middle class domestic pet, the milder and more passive animal is more suitable for its present role.

Boxers were the first breed to be used by the German army. Club members in the Munich area gave 60 dogs in 1914, complete with collars and leads, and Philip Stockmann, by then called up for military service was put in charge of their training. The dogs guarded prisoners, and escorted working parties, and also accompanied patrols searching for escaped prisoners and defectors. The dogs proved ideal for this work, quiet in action and not barking unnecessarily, not biting unless their handlers were attacked, when they were trained to leap at the back of the neck of the adversary, sometimes flooring three or four men at a time, and standing quietly over them until the soldiers could take over. These donated dogs had known all the comforts of warm homes, but they stood up well to the extreme conditions of the first winter of the war, not seeking shelter even when provided. The Boxer proved itself a professional guard dog, and opened up the way for other breeds to be used by the German army.

Before World War II, many German/Jewish people had fled to Palestine, setting up communes there with their families and their dogs, including a great many Boxers, mostly the stocky, compact dark brindles which did not have at that time the elegance of the reds. A British Army Veterinary Corps detachment recruited these dogs in World War II, and used them to accompany soldiers guarding airfields. As war dogs they were superbly courageous and one soldier with a pair of dogs could keep a whole airfield clear of intruders. Use of dogs at that time was unsophisticated, in that the dogs were allowed to attack and kill if they found unauthorised persons within the airfield perimeter. The war dogs had numbers, and records of their successes were kept. It was during World War II that many British servicemen came to admire the Boxer, and undoubtedly many were smuggled back to Britain in army trucks when hostilities ended.

It was with grandchildren of the Palestinian army dogs that I began breeding Boxers. The grandmother of Satan, my first stud dog, was recorded as having killed eleven intruders . . . but a sweeter dog to handle than Satan you have never met. This sums up the Boxer character, power and ferocity when needed, total reliability with owners, and gentleness with the young and weak.

The British Club was founded in 1936. Mr Allan Dawson imported several good dogs, including the great Zunftig Von Dom for his Stainburndorf kennel. This dog might have altered the whole course of Boxer breeding here, except that panic prevailed at the outbreak of war in 1939. People feared that they would be unable to feed their dogs if the country were devastated, so Zunftig was sold to America, and his selling price donated to the Red Cross. In the war years the kennels of the Bramblings, the Panfields, Maspounds and Cuckmeres kept the breed going, in a limited way. Dog shows were still held, but confined to entries from the local area, to save unessential use of transport.

After the war, 1946 saw 707 Boxers registered at the Kennel Club. This number doubled the next year, and the Boxer boom was on, until the breed climbed to the third most popular in Britain with 7570 registrations in 1956. Boxer puppies found a ready sale to families setting up homes, Boxer acceptance going hand in hand with the post-war rise in the birth rate of human children, the building of new homes and a situation of full employment. By the time the dogs of 1956 had died, averaging a ten-year life for the breed, registrations had settled down to about 4000 a year, and the Boxer had dropped out of the top ten most popular dogs.

Changes in the economic and social climate, even a widening of views on contraception, abortion and divorce, all militate against keeping large and demanding pets who cannot be left in homes which are empty all day. In the present economic recession, Boxer breeders were quick to realise they must cut down on litters, so there is some scarcity of Boxer pups now, but quality remains high, and many think a certain amount of difficulty in obtaining a Boxer puppy goes some way to ensuring that they go to homes which have given the purchase great consideration.

The great names in Boxer kennels rise and fall over the years, sometimes because their owners are hampered by other considerations from showing and breeding, or sometimes because a line producing winners falls, for no obvious reason, into the doldrums. In the 1950s, the famous kennels were the Panfields, the Gremlins, and the Burstalls, and the stud dog everyone wanted to see was the great Champion Winkinglight Viking, a descendant of the famous Dutch Von Haus Germania Kennel.

1956 saw the emergence of the Champion litter sisters, Wardrobes Miss Mink, and Wardrobes Miss Sable, heralding the great run of triumph for Mr and Mrs Wilson Wiley, which was to dominate British Boxerdom for more than fifteen years. In the 1960s the Wardrobes kennel was a byword. Although the Wilson Wileys were never great puppy producers themselves, they were able to see many litters by their studs and had a wonderful gift for picking a good one from a litter.

Another much used dog of the 1960s was Raineylane Sirocco, imported from USA by Mr Martin Summers, in his Summerdale partnership with Mrs Fairbrother of the Gremlin prefix. In 1968 Mrs Pat Heath's Seefield Picasso became a Champion. This dog has had immense influence on the breed since that time, as a great sire and a great showman. He also had some wins in Obedience Competition, although he never equalled the achievement of his sire, Ch. Seefield Holbein, in qualifying CD Excellent at working trials, the only Boxer Show Champion to do so.

In the mid-1970s Picasso's children and grandchildren continue the winning ways. Picasso's great rival in the beauty show ring was another outstanding dog, Champion Marbelton Desperate Dan, a spectacular dog to show and a good laster.

When the current Head Breed Warden of the German Boxer Club judged the British Club's Championship Show in 1976 he found head type much improved, but the craze for white markings on all the show dogs offended him, as these dogs look far less substantial than those with solid coloured coats.

American Boxers

The first American Boxer was registered in USA in 1904, and there was the opportunity to import several great German stud dogs during World War I, but there was not very wide interest until the American Boxer Club was founded in 1935. In 1938, numbers had increased so much that the Club was able to invite

Philip Stockmann, then Head Breed Warden of the Munich Club, to judge over a hundred Boxers. So the Americans had a headstart on Britain, which they were able to consolidate by buying good dogs from war-torn Britain and Europe during World War II, when it was extremely difficult to keep and feed dogs on this side of the Atlantic. By the generosity of American owners, both Frau Stockmann herself, and several British breeders received gifts of puppies after the war, descendants of the dogs which the Americans had paid large sums of money to take into safe keeping.

Boxers have never achieved the top ranks of popularity in America as pet dogs, and compared with Britain, relatively few are bred, but there are some large, specialist exhibitors' kennels regularly producing dogs to take the top prizes on the show circuits. American dogs, the males slightly taller than the British standard, are beautifully presented with their fashionable markings sparkling white. Professional handlers are usually employed; they have superb control over their dogs, and are only willing to take on dogs which have a fair chance of doing them credit, so American shows present more of a spectacle than a similar event in Britain.

As the ears of American Boxers are cropped, they cannot be exhibited for competition in Britain, although they are brought over as stud dogs and brood bitches at considerable expense because of the need to stay six months in quarantine kennels. European countries which permit the cropped ear can import American dogs freely. Until quite lately Finland was working almost entirely with American Boxers, but the 1971 ban on cropping opened up that country to British exports again.

Australia and New Zealand have difficulty in taking USA stock, as America has indigenous rabies, while Australia is free and intends to remain so. An American dog must spend a year in Britain before going on to Australia, so in practice, Australia gets its dogs from Britain, which with Cyprus, Hawaii, the Antarctic and Scandinavia are the only countries in the world free of rabies.

Boxer love is strong in Scandinavia, where there are no quarantine regulations between Norway, Sweden and Finland so that dogs can participate in the shows held in each country. Denmark is excluded because Danish dogs can be shown in rabies-infected Europe. In Scandinavia, the work of the judges is complicated by having cropped and natural eared dogs in the ring at the same time.

Finland seeks to retain the true temperament by insisting that a Boxer which has won one challenge certificate must pass an Obedience test before going on to win two more certificates and to qualify as a Champion. As is usual everywhere in Europe, every dog entered at a show is commented on by the judge and graded, down to the lowest rating 'zero' for an untypical specimen, or one with disqualifying faults. This method has the virtue of discouraging early on the owners of poor quality dogs, and also makes the judge's opinion quite unequivocal, unlike the British show scene where the second and third prize winners often receive ambiguous comments in the dog press, and nothing is said about the rest of the entry.

Holland has always been a stronghold of Boxers, being especially known for producing good heads. Some excellent dogs, including some of Frau

Mr and Mrs H. Wilson Wiley's Champion Wardrobes Clair de Lune holder of the breed record for 31 challenge certificates. Completed in 1973. Clair is daughter of Ch. Wardrobes Hunters Moon

Twin sister, Naiad and Folly, live as one dog

Mrs. Chris Stander's American Champion, Champion Sentry's Surge, bred by owner. From Michigan, USA

One of the few winning German Boxers now to be found without imported British blood lines. International Champion and VDH Sieger Einzie von Nahmertal, owned by Dr. R. Osterberg, of Pohlheim

17

Stockmann's went to Holland in the late 1930s, during the National Socialist rise to power. During the war years, there was of necessity a lot of close in-breeding, fixing the type. Dutch imports, particularly those from the Von Haus Germania kennel, did a lot for the breed in Britain after World War II.

For many British breeders, the height of achievement was reached when a British Boxer, Mrs Wither's Witherford Hot Chestnut, became the first Boxer puppy to go back to Germany, the homeland of its breed. Chestnut had his ears cropped there, and was later shown all over Europe, becoming a World Champion. Even more important was his prepotency as a sire, for he produced 35 more Champions and many more big winners, so that in one year, one third of all the Boxers registered in Germany were traceable to Chestnut. This great Boxer gentleman lived to be thirteen and a half years old, a splendid dog and an unforgettable tribute to British Boxer breeding.

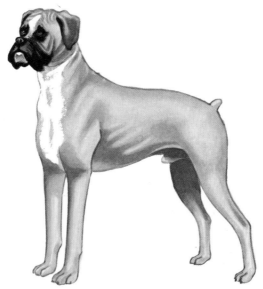

A fawn male with a good black mask

The breed standard

The first task of the pioneer enthusiasts of any breed is to formulate the breed standard, the pattern of physical qualities and characteristics which represents their ideal. The approved standard is retained by the Kennel Club of the country; in many breeds the standards differ, as the American and British ones do in respect of height of the male, and the cropping of ears.

At a dog show, the judge should evaluate the dogs with the breed standard in mind, and in theory, the dog most approximating to it must win, but in practice it will be found that even the most explicit wording is interpreted differently by each individual, and it is extremely difficult to frame a description of the features of a dog in precise wording. It took the Munich Boxer Club six years to devise their standard and to get it agreed, but then they were really designing a dog, a truly man-made breed.

One of the first things to decide was colour. Whites and checks were ruled out, as unsuitable for police and army dogs; the blacks went largely because their owner was unpopular. This left red, in shades from fawn to deep deer red, and the brindles, which have well defined black stripes on a red ground. Dogs with very widely spaced stripes on clear red are known as 'tiger brindles'; those with stripes much closer together giving a darker effect are called 'mahogany brindles.' In each case the ground should be golden or red, and the stripes should not run together.

The mask should be black, unless there are white markings. (White must not in any case exceed one third of the dog's colour.) In Europe generally, markings approaching the permitted one third are frowned on, but British show dogs need to have flashy markings.

Both the British and American standards of the Boxer are based on the original German. They are very full, seeking to define every feature, and sometimes losing a little clarity in the translation.

The full standards may be obtained for a small fee from the Kennel Club of each country, or from Boxer breed clubs. It will be sufficient if we look at the essential specification for Boxer excellence in summarised form, bearing in mind that the standard refers to the adult dog of about two years upwards; up to that age the Boxer does a lot of changing, particularly in the shape of the head.

The character stipulated in the standard is that the Boxer should be distrustful of strangers, but this only becomes true when the dog is adult. Up to that time, the Boxer should be boisterously friendly with everyone. Most dogs acquire the necessary reserve with adult status, but some bitches go on being fulsomely and indiscriminately affectionate all their lives, but still seem able to alter their bearing instantly in time of need. Never mistrust your Boxer's guard instincts. There are very few which are not born guard dogs.

In general appearance, the Boxer is a medium-sized, well muscled, smooth coated dog of square figure and strong limbs. The Boxer should never be plump or heavy, ribs should just show when a deep breath is taken. In Britain, the weight of a typical male should be about 65 lb. (26kg.); weight is not specified in the American standard. British heights are males: 22-24in. (55-60cm.) at point of shoulder (withers); bitches: 21-23in. (53-58cm.). A typical bitch of middle height should weigh 62lb. (24kg.). The American male height should fall within the limits: 22½-25in. (56-65cm.); American bitches: 21-23½in. (52.5-59cm.).

The long strong muscles rippling under the skin when the Boxer moves is one of its attractions. The skin should not be close-packed with tissue.

The Boxer must move energetically, with a firm, purposeful stride, head held high, proudly, with a degree of arrogance. The eyes should be dark brown, not deepset, but not bulging, lively and bright, not limpid and sad.

The ears should be small and thin, set at the highest point of the side of the skull, lying flat against the cheek, or falling forward with a definite crease when alert. Untidy ears are a most common fault. In USA the size of ear is not important, as they will be cropped when the puppy is about three months old.

The mouth should be wide, the six incisor teeth in a straight line, and of course, the mouth is undershot, the lower jaw which must be level extending beyond the upper. A wry mouth is a very bad fault to breed from. Once the breed was plagued with them, but they are now much rarer. The wry mouth allows teeth to protrude, and often the tongue to be permanently extended. This is ugly, and makes for slobbering.

The head, which is such a distinctive feature of the breed, is shown on P.23 more clearly than is possible in words.

The neck is a great feature of nobility and beauty for too short a neck gives the dog a cloddy, coarse appearance. The neck of good length, muscular and elegantly arched down to the back, enabled the fighting dog to maintain a steady grip. You will find your own Boxer can do the same movement, showing great agility by just head turning, when you are trying to recover your best bedroom slippers.

The chest should be deep, reaching to the elbows, half the height of the dog, and there should be a definite, graceful slope up to the loins, which should not be light and greyhound-like, but slim and lithe.

The front legs are straight and powerful; the large, muscular thighs are well rounded, and well angulated hip and knee joints give powerful propulsion. Straight back legs are a major fault, both for showing and for free movement, and they look very ugly. Feet are small, rounded with tightly arched toes on which the Boxer rests lightly. Long, hare-like feet are frequently seen, but they ruin the appearance. Feet can be improved by walking on hard pavements, but the really long foot cannot be altered in this way.

The back should be broad and strong, neither roached up nor hollowed. The cropped tail, about 2in. (5cm.) long in the adult, should be set high, and carried erect. The habit handlers have of holding up the tail when posing dogs in the show ring is to be deplored.

In 1975 the World Small Animal Veterinary Congress unanimously passed a resolution to ban all unnecessary mutilation of animals; this included ear cropping, tail docking, elective hysterectomy and castration. Within the veterinary profession there is some dissension about implementing this resolution, which is not yet mandatory, for not all vets feel that this question

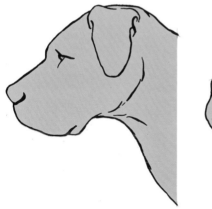

Too long

Too bull-doggy

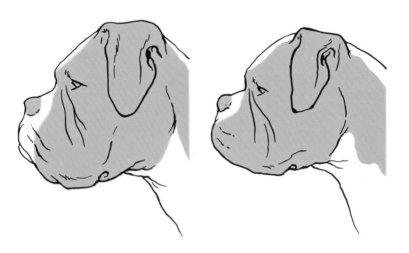

The modern male and female type head

Common faults of the Boxer head

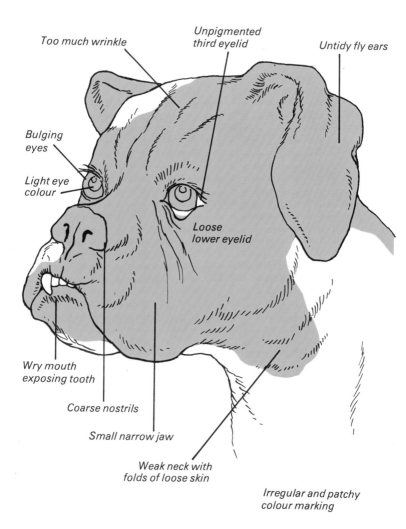

Too much wrinkle

Unpigmented
third eyelid

Untidy fly ears

Bulging
eyes

Light eye
colour

Loose
lower eyelid

Wry mouth
exposing tooth

Coarse nostrils

Small narrow jaw

Weak neck with
folds of loose skin

Irregular and patchy
colour marking

Good modern male head

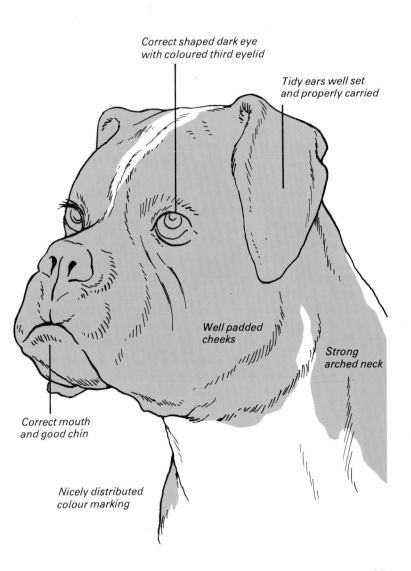

Correct shaped dark eye
with coloured third eyelid

Tidy ears well set
and properly carried

Well padded
cheeks

Strong
arched neck

Correct mouth
and good chin

Nicely distributed
colour marking

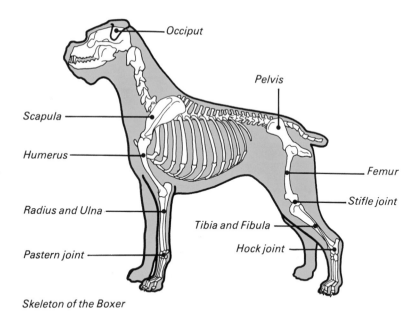

Skeleton of the Boxer

Labels: Occiput, Pelvis, Scapula, Humerus, Femur, Radius and Ulna, Stifle joint, Tibia and Fibula, Pastern joint, Hock joint

merits priority at present, as relatively little suffering is involved. Some vets will go on performing these operations if clients request them, as it is often in the long term for the benefit of the dog. It may be argued that even tail docking and ear cropping fall within the description of benefits, since the sales of a puppy would be prejudiced if it did not conform to current fashion.

Boxer exhibitors in Britain are not in favour of a ban on docking. They feel the whole balance of the dog would be altered and we should have to get an eye in for a totally different silhouette. Any ban on tail docking imposed by the veterinary profession would have only minor effect as most docking is done quite legally by breeders, before the pup's eyes are open, usually at three or four days when the pain threshold is high. No anaesthetic is needed, and the cutting does not worry the pup overmuch. Front leg dew claws are removed at the same time; I have never seen a Boxer with hind dew claws.

Ear cropping is definitely a matter for the vet, as a full anaesthetic is needed. **Timing is important; it is usually done between twelve and sixteen weeks,** when the ears begin to lift. Ear cropping surgeons tend to be specialists as considerable artistry is needed to get the ears balanced, and to suit each head. Templates are sometimes used in USA, and after cutting, the ears are supported on cones of wire or plaster until the edges have healed. The pups

24

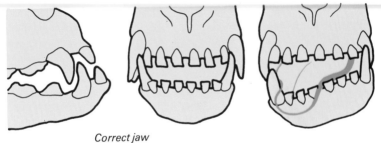

Correct jaw

Wry mouth and protruding tongue

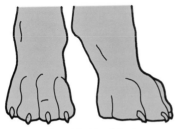

Tight well-padded 'cat' feet

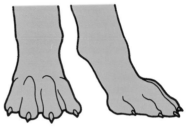

Incorrect elongated spread foot

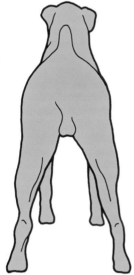

Correct stance with well-muscled thighs and up on toes

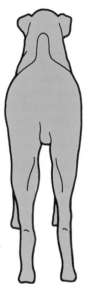

Close behind lacking in muscle and propulsion power

25

are usually kept under mild sedation for a few days while healing takes place.

The male must have two testicles descended into the scrotum.

It is not at all easy to breed a Boxer with all the attributes approaching those demanded in the standard. As an example of the way inherited tendencies come through, I am permitted, by the kindness of the editors of the magazine *Boxerama* to reprint an extract from an article by Frau Stockmann, first written for the German magazine *Boxer Blätter*. The Mendelian theory of inheritance is explained as follows: 'Take two Boxers with dominant faults. A owns a very good bitch, whose only fault is that she is straight in stifle (knee joint). In order to get rid of this fault, he takes her to B who owns a dog with a good turn of stifle, but a roached (arched) back; hoping that these two animals will complement each other. As these faults are both dominant, the majority of puppies will show both these faults, but in the second daughter generation, these types will segregate again. There will be four types: a Boxer with roach back but good in turn of stifle; a Boxer with flat top line but a straight stifle; a Boxer with a roach and a straight stifle, and at last, a Boxer with a good back and good quarters.'

The odds on getting one puppy with neither of the parent's faults are, alas, greater than a one-in-three chance, as Mendelian theory proves that 25% of pups will show characteristics of the sire, 25% characteristics of the dam, and 50% will have their inheritance in mixed form. To continue with Frau Stockmann's article: 'We have seen that the individual offspring produce quite differently; that two different types remain pure, and two segregate which gives us sixteen different hereditary factors. Divide the roach backed, straight stifled Boxers among sixteen, and bear in mind the dominance of the faults; the following will be the result: nine Boxers straight behind and roached; three Boxers straight behind but with good level backs; three Boxers good behind but roached; one Boxer good behind and with good back. The Breeder can console himself that one dog, which bears the two recessive characteristics, will breed true. One of each of the other four types will breed true as well, but which one that will be is impossible to tell.

Three factors decide the actual breeding value of an animal: (a) the appearance; (b) the pedigree; (c) the type of progeny it throws. The latter is of prime importance, particularly in the second daughter generation.'

Let us return to the instance already quoted, but in place of the straight stifle, take the light eye, and instead of roached back, a dog that shows its teeth. These are faults which in my opinion are passed on as hidden characteristics. Thus we have the following result: nine Boxers with dark eyes and normal mouths; three Boxers with dark eyes but showing their teeth; three Boxers with light eyes but good mouths; one Boxer with light eyes and showing its teeth. Of the nine Boxers with dark eyes and good mouths, only one will breed progeny without these faults, the other eight, despite their apparent faultless appearance, and the same breeding, will pass on the faults, or at least have a tendency to do so. Neither appearance nor pedigree is the deciding factor in assessing the breeding value of an animal, but the progeny it throws.

The pedigree, so much valued by new owners for its length and splattering of red ink, is of little value unless you can picture the dogs which produced

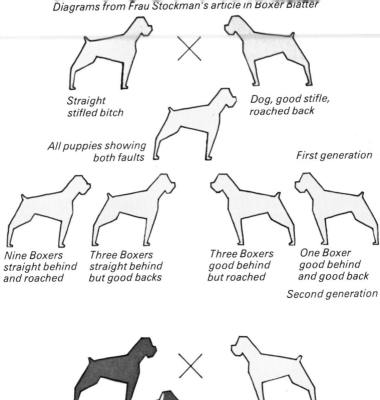

Straight
stifled bitch

Dog, good stifle,
roached back

All puppies showing
both faults

First generation

Nine Boxers
straight behind
and roached

Three Boxers
straight behind
but good backs

Three Boxers
good behind
but roached

One Boxer
good behind
and good back

Second generation

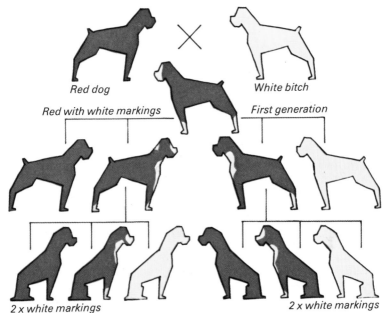

Red dog

White bitch

Red with white markings

First generation

2 x white markings

2 x white markings

27

yours. The most famous dogs will be illustrated in breed books and annuals; the less illustrious and the hardworking brood bitches are likely to be known only by their owners. If you wish to research into the background of your dog it is essential to buy from a breeder who knows the line well and can help you from a private collection of photographs. This research is time-consuming, and really only necessary if you mean to breed litters, with a view to keeping a better specimen. It is extraordinary how often new owners will mate a quite nice bitch to the leading sire of the day, and then be very disappointed that totally beautiful progeny did not result. The litter is always lovely and it is only when the next generation is adult that the faults show up.

A fine upstanding dog with red and white markings

Choosing a puppy

Buying

All the family should be involved in buying the Boxer, but on the first visits to see puppies, it is best to keep the party small, ideally to two adults, as if you take children with you, you may be stampeded into buying unwisely. Do not hesitate to visit several breeders, so that you can compare litters, adults and surroundings, and both human and dog personalities, but be a little tactful and do not talk about one to another, and do not make any commitments which may be interpreted as firm ones, so holding up the sale of a puppy to another home.

If you do find a puppy you like, put a deposit of about one third of the purchase price down quickly, as the optimum selling time for Boxers is quite short, between six and nine weeks of age, so the breeder will quite reasonably want to sell to the first people who, in his opinion, fulfil the standard for Boxer owners. You may be slightly surprised to find that you, the buyer, are assuming the unfamiliar role in being subjected to an interview to see if you are suitable to own a Boxer. In the end it works to your advantage, in that experienced breeders can see where the people or the home is going to fail to stand the Boxer strain, even though you feel enchanted with the idea of having a puppy.

Many people who would dearly love a Boxer have to accept that they must take an easier dog. Being told that a breeder does not want to sell you a puppy may be hurtful, even offensive at the time, but it could save you a lot of expense and heartbreak in the end. Boxer breeders want to sell puppies, but to their everlasting credit, the majority will only sell where the dog will be happy. One of the saddest cases for refusal is when people have had a lifetime of enjoyable Boxer ownership, and then come looking for another puppy, failing to face the fact that they are now too elderly or frail to take on another energetic youngster, for it is all too easy to forget what a Boxer adolescent can be like, when the recent experience has been with a placid older dog. Sometimes we are able to bring such people together with a displaced adult dog, a happy solution for them all.

When you have decided that you mean to buy, all the family should visit to familiarise themselves with the pup and its dam. All the immediate household should be included, but please do not use the ride as an opportunity to pay off social obligations, so that you bring all the relations and the children to whom you owe a treat. Nothing antagonises breeders so much as being used as a cheap version of a domestic zoo. This is a very serious purchase you are making, a lot of talking has to be done, and uninvolved people and children are a distraction for both buyer and seller. Oddly enough, we find that people who are normally extremely discriminating when buying a car or a household appliance seem to lose all critical ability when buying a pup. You must make absolutely sure that it is in good working order!

In buying a pedigree Boxer from a breeder, you have the right to expect that the pedigree is correct, and applies to the puppy that you buy. There is no positive check on this in Britain. The Kennel Club can check that a pedigree is possible, but not that it applies to a particular animal. In Canada all puppies have an identification mark, and it is not unusual to buy the puppy, and then to pay extra for its pedigree later if it is wanted for showing or breeding.

In Britain, since April 1976 all puppies must be registered into the Litter recording category before they are four weeks old. Extra puppies cannot be included in a litter registration later. The pups may then be registered individually by name, either by the breeder or the purchaser, into the Basic Register, from which they must be transferred into the Active Register before showing or breeding is undertaken. Registrations sometimes take some weeks to come through, so may not be available when you collect your puppy.

Your puppy should have been fed and reared for maximum health, and there should be no physical and mental defects in the line which the breeder is aware of, or could be aware of, if the relative tests had been made. The puppy should have been adequately wormed, tail docked and dew claws removed, and prepared for life as a companion to people. A detailed diet sheet and worming certificate should be provided with the puppy and the breeder should be prepared, to give advice after you have the pup in your home.

If there is any dispute about health when you collect your puppy, a veterinary surgeon's decision should be final, if obtained within twenty-four hours and your deposit should be returned in full if the puppy is not in good health. In any other circumstance, deposits are lost if you fail to conclude the bargain by the time the pup should leave home and you have not let the breeder know why. If you require primary vaccination of the puppy before it leaves the breeder, this will always be extra to the purchase price, and will probably involve the cost of a veterinary surgeon's visit.

You should be allowed to see all the puppies in a litter, even those already reserved, so that you can make comparison. You must see the dam or the sire. Boxer mums can look rather run down after rearing a big litter, sometimes their coat comes off in patches, and the mammary glands will be hanging down, perhaps looking scratched and red, and the bitch may be a bit thin, but your natural judgement will tell you whether this is a well cared for Boxer lady, coming to the end of a big task, or whether she is worried, underfed and dirty. If you see the pups at three weeks the dam may be a little wary, protective of her brood, and even growly.

As the weeks go on, she should be more relaxed, willing to leave the pups more often, ready to have a word with visitors. Once the pups are on their feet, the bitch will let you handle them, but she may come close, nudging your arm, intimating 'be careful with my baby'. You may find the bitch is away from the puppies altogether, busy recovering her figure and getting fattened up again. Some exhibitors remove bitches from litters far too early, with the idea of getting them back into the show ring quickly, but this is not a good start in life for the puppy, even if feeding is adequately supplemented.

The choice of the puppy from the litter must always be a personal thing, the one you are immediately attracted to. Do not be misled by 'the quiet one' for it may have been roaring about five minutes before. The bold extrovert male usually shows up at about five weeks old. In the Boxer, such an animal may be quite a handful later, and will require a strongly dominant owner to control it in adolescent days. It is usual to find one specially agile pup, the one that can see the way out of the playpen, climbs like a monkey up the wire, topples over to freedom, again and again, for once they have found the way, they seldom unlearn it. This bundle of energy and ingenuity, can you endure it? Only you can size up your own capabilities and find the pup to suit you. You may admire the great intelligence of your pup, and enjoy developing the Boxer's clever ways, or you may opt for a quieter life with a duller but more docile pup.

If you have owned a Boxer before, by all means take the pedigree to show the seller of your new friend, as it may be interesting to see where the breeding lines link up, but please do not take a photograph of the old favourite, and insist on matching up colour and markings. Many breeders will be reluctant to sell to you if you do this, as it indicates that you are trying to re-create another dog's personality and it will handicap you in the acceptance of the new puppy as a dog in its own right.

It is extremely hard not to yearn for a well-loved dog to come back. I am always looking for my old Pixie, who was, and always will be, my best dog in the world. I see glimpses of her in great grand-daughter Pooka, in great, great grandson Tigger, and in other people's dogs which are not at all related, but there never will be another Pixie, even with the same bloodlines to breed from. It is perfectly understandable that you want another red, or a brindle with or without white markings, but when you get down to wanting to match the length of the socks, the exact streak of white on the head, then we conclude you are not yet ready for a new puppy. All Boxers do some of the same things, but their characters are as varied as those of human beings; that is the charm of the breed.

The age at which you collect your puppy rather depends on your own inclinations and commitments. The strong out-going male pup can leave as early as six weeks old, provided it is eating its food quite independently of the dam, is adventurous and bold, and the new owner has plenty of time to spend with the puppy. I would let a pup of this age go to a mature family with few social obligations, where the woman was maternal and really wanted to enjoy having a dog very dependent on her at first. A pup as young as this should not go to a noisy household, one that does a lot of entertaining, or where the children are of less than teenage. Quiet and plenty of undisturbed rest is essential for the pup. It is only to be expected that children will want to enjoy their puppy when they have it, so a nine-week-old puppy will be much more suitable for them.

Eight weeks used to be the traditional time for collecting puppies, but just lately dog psychologists have told us that eight weeks in a dog equates with the eight-month 'fear period' in a human baby, and it is not a good stage to make changes in environment. Boxer pups age quickly, and by twelve weeks they can be real little hooligans, up to any mischief, so it is really desirable to get them into your home, and learning where they fit into the scheme of things, before that age. Boxer pups need to get civilised early, while they are young enough to listen to what you tell them. Pups which stay on in kennels after twelve weeks become rough, strong-willed and increasingly hard to teach.

Pups should be collected about mid-morning, well after the breakfast has gone down, to avoid sickness on the first journey. Two people should come to collect, so that the pup may be held securely in someone's arms for this first journey outside its home; this pays good dividends in having a confident dog later, the policy being to avoid all frights in these early days. Pups are paid for in full when collected. It is very important to keep the puppy on the same food, and the same feeding schedule during the first days in its new home.

A male puppy bought as a stud dog or for exhibition will need to have a veterinary check as assurance that two testicles are present and likely to descend into the scrotum. The testicles may be down at eight weeks, but in the very young male, testicles react very strongly to the fight or flight syndrome, and may be retracted into the body. If being 'entire' is going to matter to you, veterinary examination is your safeguard, but not an absolute insurance. Dogs with only one testicle descended, (unilateral cryptochids, or mono-orchids) are fertile, and may be exhibited, but most judges would regard this as a major fault.

People have been known to want to return a puppy after the first night of ownership, because the pup cried, puddled on the carpet, or tore the newspaper. This reveals only too clearly that the whole idea of having a puppy was not properly thought out and discussed, and the breeder will rightly be angry, although most will take the puppy back for the sake of the dog. The usual system is to re-sell the puppy and refund your purchase price, less any extra expenses for boarding and re-advertising. It is sad, but true, that the value of Boxer puppies drops alarmingly after twelve weeks. Some buyers declare a pup of this age 'too old' as by then they believe they will have missed the pleasure of the little baby days. The three-month Boxer is altering in head, becoming thin and leggy, and increasingly headstrong and mischievous. If you return a puppy at three months or older, its selling prospects are comparatively low, and the original price you paid will not be recovered, so this is just one more reason for being sure before buying.

The choice of sex of your Boxer is much more important than colour or markings. In the larger breeds, the characters of dog and bitch are quite dissimilar, so it is almost impossible to be indifferent about the sex you want to own. A Boxer bitch might be ideal for your family, when the male might be too big and forceful. On the other hand the hormonal cycle of the bitch may be inconvenient to you.

The Boxer male should be distinguishable at a glance from the female, not only sexually, but by size and masculinity of bearing. The bitch is by no means a small animal, but should be feminine in appearance. Bitches are softer in character, more demonstrative and sympathetic to their owners, and in general, not so defiant of authority. The bitch will do as you say to please you, the dog because it respects you. A generalisation I agree, but truer more often than not. I like the devotion of the Boxer bitch, my husband likes the size and spirit of the male. When a Boxer is being bought for a young family, with children to be taken out in pram or push chair, the bitch is the better choice, for the young male can be too strong. Bitches are very kind to little children, while dogs are great company for young men and middle-aged families.

What litters look like

When people set out to buy a companion dog, knowing they will never have the time or inclination to enter the show circuit, they so often say, 'We don't want a good one', when they mean precisely the opposite. Everyone wants a properly reared, healthy puppy, without physical and mental disabilities, and they want it to look reasonably like a Boxer, otherwise they might as well buy a crossbred. The 'good one', that is, the one likely to be noticed in the show ring, will only be distinguishable at puppy stage by very well balanced conformation and smart markings. For such a showing prospect, you would expect to pay, at seven to nine weeks old, perhaps 25% more than the price of companion puppies.

So much can happen to alter the prospects of the show puppy that it is impossible to predict a winner at this stage. Markings do not alter very much, except that some white hair seems to be lost, but the plain red or brindle puppy will never acquire more white. An over-white marked face will not darken, either.

If you are interested in showing in Britain or USA, white markings equal on each side of the face, round the collar, and on the socks, a nice leavening on the rich red or well defined brindle coat, is desirable, but beware of the very flashy puppy which may in the end run close to having over a third white, and will also breed a large proportion of whites if mated to a dog with similar markings.

The skull of the puppy should be domed at this age, the eyes dark blue, clear and bright, and the skin glossy and loose on the body. For your companion pup, the physical features should be the same, but you can be perfectly content with a plainer brindle or red, the type which would be showable in Europe, or you may be satisfied with unbalanced markings.

Light eyes can alter the expression very much, and may not ever please you. At six to eight weeks you get a fleeting glimpse of the mature dog but after this such rapid growth takes place, and the head begins to change as the second teeth come through, that every Boxer inevitably goes through a plain and gangly stage. Some Boxers do not reach their peak until they are four, so be prepared for a long ugly duckling stage. Dogs which mature early, or have weight put on them by cramming, to please the owner's eye, very soon become heavy and coarse. The fit and active Boxer, between twelve and twenty-four months, can look to the uninformed eye, too thin. Naiad and Folly have always looked like animated anatomical diagrams until just recently, because they were too active to accumulate fat.

The puppy you choose must be healthy. Please harden your heart against buying from pity; it is always a mistake. We are fortunate that animals can be painlessly destroyed if they have a physical or mental infirmity, and this is the only solution for an ailing puppy. Years ago I used to be proud of having reared a puppy that was weak, but I would not do it again. It is not fair to the buyer, as such a puppy may always be more vulnerable to illness and disease, and may have a shortened life through some defect. I would like you to have great personal pride in the dog you choose, having no need to apologise for its looks.

When people admire Pooka, I am always quick to point out that she is mismarked. So often the reply is, 'Mismarked where?' although to me the half white face is all too evident. I am trying to stop myself denigrating her in this way. It would be unbearably hurtful to be so quick to point out the physical faults in a human friend.

I hope you will never agree to buy a puppy that has running eyes, or nose, diarrhoea, leg weakness, badly turned in feet, or red soreness around the genitals, denoting urine scalding which can be a dreadful nuisance in the young bitch. I once had a puppy with persistent 'nappy rash' through a malformed vulva, and despite treatment, she had to be put down at a year old. Boxers are not, as a breed, often born with umbilical or inguinal hernias, but it is as well to check as the inguinal hernia will require operation later on.

The all white, or the check puppy will make a good pet if you do not mind the colour, provided it is not congenitally deaf for this factor goes with lack of pigment. Deafness can be tested at about six weeks old, not by calling, but by dropping a metal food dish behind the puppy. The deaf puppy has no future at all, it will always be a danger to itself and others. Most breeders will put their white puppies down at birth, because of the risk of deafness and because they cannot be registered at the Kennel Club, and are therefore ineligible for breeding or showing. Moreover, they are not much credit to their sire, and some breeders would rather forget that whites are born into their line.

Whites are not albinos. They usually have dark eyes and noses and for some reason they are often the largest of the litter and have very good body shape. Unless I am absolutely sure of buyers for my whites, I put them down immediately they are born, as whites command a minimal price, and we feel that the cheap dog is often the discarded dog when puppy days are over. This somewhat cynical view is borne out by the number of white animals which come into Boxer rescue schemes.

If you want a white puppy then you must be of very good faith, and order before birth, and the same criteria applies to puppies with full length tails, which again, are not typical as the show regulations now stand. If you want to pioneer the long tails, be prepared to pay the full purchase price of the puppy at three days old, when it would otherwise be docked.

If you want to have the ears left in natural state in a 'cropping' country, then you have until two to three months to make up your mind. Cropping of the ears can be done when the dog is more mature, but tail docking done later is a major operation which is difficult to heal, although badly docked tails are sometimes re-docked later on.

Boxer puppies are relatively small when born, and litter sizes can be quite large, tens and twelves, although the modern tendency is more usually fives or sixes, so perhaps fertility is dropping all round.

At birth pups will weigh about 10oz. (250g.) and will be a mousy grey-brown in appearance, except of course for the whites. When they are thoroughly dry, it is possible for the practised eye to pick out which will be brindle and which red, although it is possible to be deceived about the red which develops very light 'tiger' brindling when the fluffy puppy coat is shed. Very young puppies in the nest seem to have more white markings than is apparent when they are on their feet and some of the chest and stomach white is hidden. The muzzles are all pink, the nose and mask blacken later.

The pups are almost sugar-mouse shape, with blunt head and rounded body. Eyes are tightly closed, merely a line, ears are laid back against the head, and the aural orifice closed.

Deformities and malformations are not uncommon when nature is so bountiful. They may be hereditary, (from ancestors, not necessarily the immediate parents) or congenital due to some infection or overcrowding in the uterus, or there may be injuries at birth or just after, when the bitch is cleaning the puppies. Pups are born with deformities of the limbs, flattened rib cages, imperforate anus, or cleft palates . . . the last easily discernible when the milk returns down the nose of the puppy. It is not unusual for a Boxer bitch to squash one or two puppies in the early days before they are strong enough to wriggle away when she flops down on them. The extremely excitable or very harassed bitch may lick her pups so constantly that she removes the abdominal skin, but this is uncommon in the Boxer.

Eyes begin to open at seven to ten days and the pups will start to respond to sound at about eighteen to twenty days, rather earlier than some breeds. At twenty-one days the pups should be getting to their feet, somewhat uncertainly, depending a good deal on the floor surface. Breeders frequently rear pups on newspaper for cleanliness, but it does provide a difficult surface to get a grip on.

Unless you are specially privileged, and a good friend of the Boxer bitch, you will be unlikely to see puppies before they are three weeks old. Until this time, they and the dam need peace and seclusion in a room well away from noise and alarms, warm and shaded from strong light. If you do get a peep at bitch and litter, you will find the dam that has had a good whelping, and is satisfied with her surroundings and free from pain, stretched out on her side, so that the pups can feed, just lifting her head and turning the neck to clean the pups. One or two pups that are not feeding at the time will be cuddled under the neck. The back two teats have the best supply of milk and are most in demand, but the pups latch on to any one they can find. They do not appropriate a special teat and keep exclusively to it, as some authorities state. Naturally the strongest pups get the best choice.

At twenty-one days of age comes the first big step into the world for pups, for this has been found, by scientific experiment to be the best period for socialisation, when really permanent imprints are made on the little dog's brain. Now the puppies are ready for handling. They can enjoy a sunny room, having been unable until now to take strong light, but they may still object to being in full light outdoors. They will also be ready to lap. The dam will still be feeding the pups, but they will be on small exploratory amounts of other foods, and as soon as they can walk, the pups will be leaving their bed to pass faeces and urine as far away as they can get, instead of having the dam clean it up at source, as it were. The good Boxer mum will still clean up her puppies, though she will stop consuming the excreta, but she will have a bigger overall job, as pups often fall into their food dishes and come up covered in gruel.

When you see three-week-old puppies, the ideal place to find them is in a downstairs room, or in a kennel very near the house, where they can see and be seen frequently as people go about their business. Pups not adequately handled, talked to, and afforded the opportunity to hear household noises, music, and bangs, will never be quite so well adjusted as companions. Pups reared completely away from human influence have been found, by American research work, to become quite wild by the time they are three months old. Early conditioning once missed cannot be supplied later, however much you try.

The pups and their surroundings should be clean. They may have dirtied their newspaper, but it is easy to tell if scrubbing has been done regularly, if paper and blankets are changed quite often and if the premises are well kept and free from smell. Any home which houses dogs in quantity is liable to be a bit chewed and shabby but ideally a breeder's premises should look as if it had been furnished with a view to rational dog keeping, with easily cleaned floors, covers and curtains, so that dogs can be allowed some family life.

From three weeks old the pups will be increasingly independent of the dam's feeding, but she should have access to them, for cleaning purposes and also for tuition in the art of being a dog. Puppies which are reared completely away from the bitch do not learn to comport themselves among other dogs, and so may be shy or aggressive, and may also refuse to take up the appropriate sexual role at mating time. A nice balance of human and dog company is the best environment of all.

Worming against *toxocara canis* i.e. roundworm should start at three weeks, and the process repeated at fortnightly intervals until the pups leave the breeder, when instructions should be given about further worming. It is prudent to make enquiry about the worming routine, and to be particular about handwashing when handling pups of this age, as *toxocara* has a slight, but significant risk of transference to humans.

Pups of this age sleep a good deal, in between bouts of being groomed by the dam, and grooming each other. If they get bitten too hard, or squashed, they will scream loudly. A more plaintive cry becomes easily recognisable, meaning pups are too hot, too cold, or in too bright a light, and this cry occasionally comes from a pup left outside the family group. If the bitch fails to gather in the same pup on many occasions, it is an indication that the pup has something radically wrong with it.

At four weeks old, the pups should be walking much more steadily, eyes should be able to focus well, the ears should be much more developed, and some hearing will be present. Docked tails will be healed, navels too, and the first spiky teeth are through.

Around this time you will hear the first bark. It usually frightens the pup that made it more than anyone else. It is endearing when, as often happens, I go into the pups' room in the morning and get a sharp little warning bark, as if to say, 'This is our room. Keep out!' This elementary taste of self-preservation soon evaporates. Older pups seldom bark until they are over one year, and the real house guard instinct develops. At four weeks the pups will all be going away from the nest to defecate, and they should be able to balance on their haunches nicely for this action. The dam has by now stopped cleaning them, but some Boxer mums vomit their own food for their pups in imitation of a dog living wild. Around this time the dam stands up when the pups feed. At first the pups will sit and stretch their necks up; later they will stand to feed and later still they will be scampering after their dam to snatch the last drops of milk on the run.

The puppies will have begun to play in typical Boxer style, patting with their front paws, rolling and biting at each other's ears and necks. They are extremely noisy when playing, barking and roaring at the tops of their voices. This phase soon passes; older dogs are silent in play. Active periods are quite short, fifteen to twenty minutes are quite enough, balanced by two or three hours of deep sleep from which the pups are not easily roused, and indeed they should not be, just to please visitors. Sleep is very necessary to their physical and mental development. The constantly agitated puppy grows up full of tension.

The fluffy puppy coat is beginning to go, and the true colouring will be evident. Black spots will appear on the pink nose, and these spots finally run together to make the black nasal plane, completed at about three months. Flesh coloured spots remaining are not desirable and are a show fault.

At this stage you may be making a final choice from the litter. Do not choose the puppy which consistently remains in the nest when the others come out to play, or a whiney puppy, or a lame one, or one with thin shoulders and hindquarters but a fat, pendulous belly, a harelip, or a pup much smaller than its fellows. I have reared a couple of half-sized Boxers, and very attractive they seemed at the time, but failure to grow on frequently means a heart defect or some fault in metabolism, and leads to a very short life. Beware also of the pup with an ultra-short bulldoggy face. It may have an elongated soft palate and congestion at the back of nose and throat which will be a handicap all its life. We do not see as much of this deformity now as we did years ago, for it has been largely bred out.

Once again, and no apologies for repetition, do not take the puppy you are sorry for. It is easier to turn aside from it now than when it has been part of your family for a while, and you have nursed it and paid its bills. Do not submit to the blackmail of, 'It will be put down if you do not take it.' Euthanasia properly administered by a veterinary surgeon is quite painless and free from apprehension to the puppy. We have to think of the quality of life being offered, not just the need to keep everything that is born alive. In some cases, the sickly puppy can be a disease risk to children, a target for aggression by other dogs, and always an unwarranted expense, so the mercy comes in making an early decision that it has no future.

From four weeks onwards Boxer pups grow rapidly, gaining something like 16 oz. (400g.) each week, making a weight of about 10lb. (4kg.) when they leave the breeder at around eight weeks. When pups start to get adventurous, little accidents can happen, legs and backs can be injured by a fall. If this happens, let the breeder keep the pup until it is absolutely strong again, and has been given a certificate of health by a veterinary surgeon.

At about the age of eight weeks, some disabilities make themselves apparent which were not suspected before, as at this time the puppy puts all its body systems to the test. One puppy I sold began to vomit large amounts of its food a few minutes after eating. After making due allowance for strangeness, excitement and different food, the vomiting still went on, and proved by X-ray examination to be caused by an imperfection of the outlet valve in the stomach, which was operable, but a big ordeal for such a young puppy. A deformity of the front or back legs may also become apparent when the puppy bears more weight, and at this time you may become aware of blindness, a brain defect, or an internal abnormality, or perhaps intolerance to some foods giving rise to constant diarrhoea.

Do not feel that the breeder concealed this trouble from you. Life in the puppy nest with the dam tends to obscure individual failings. For instance, a puppy with defective sight can follow by scent in familiar surroundings, and the deaf one watches its fellows. The disabilities mentioned are not common, nor are they exclusive to the Boxer, but serve to point out that the pup's grip on life, even at a rumbustious eight weeks, is fairly tenuous.

I have referred throughout to the breeder, assuming that you will buy your Boxer from the place where it was born, taking it out of the care of its Boxer mum. The only sensible variation is that you might buy from the owner of the sire, as sometimes there is an agreement to let the stud dog owner have one or two puppies. In either of these cases you will surely see one of the parents, and possibly both. You may be able to make contact with the stud dog by visiting a show at which he is exhibited.

It is difficult to understand why anyone should want to buy a 'a pig in a poke', such as a puppy whose antecedents are an unknown quantity, although written out for you on a sheet of paper which really conveys nothing about the

A very promising sturdy eight-week-old puppy

actual dogs. It is so important to see the parents, perhaps grandparents and the person who owns them and knows their ways, and was present when the puppy was born. Nearly all breeders are interested in the future of their stock and like to keep in touch with buyers, advising and helping all the days of a dog's life.

If you buy from a dealer, and pick a puppy from a box of assorted similar ones, you forfeit so many advantages in buying an unknown quantity, with no background information and no setting by which you may judge the way the pup has been reared and conditioned. Do not delude yourself that you can make up for everything once you have the puppy. Proper rearing and exercise of the pregnant bitch, good feeding during lactation, and sensitive handling through baby days make happy, affectionate Boxer puppies. The worthwhile breeder, proud of the family stock, always sells pups individually to new owners.

One special handicap to the dealer's dog will be that it may have made long journeys, two or three hundred miles across country from isolated places where pups are difficult to sell, to centres of dense population. Such a journey, boxed up with other pups, is at best traumatic for a six-week-old pup, and is also an opportunity for acquiring infection that any one of the other litters which accompany it could have. The Boxer is such a sensitive dog, for all its swagger and bluff, and it should always be accompanied by humans through any ordeal. Some good, happy and healthy pups are bought from dealers, but I see no reason to deprive yourself of the pleasure of knowing your Boxer's family background and having the breeder available to turn to as a friend.

People shop for puppies at dealers for two reasons, the 'sorry for' we have already mentioned, and the 'must have it today' syndrome. Dealers nearly always have puppies, but to get the best from a breeder you frequently have to wait. British Boxer breeders have responded especially well to cutting puppy production knowing that present conditions make it hard to accommodate a demanding breed like the Boxer.

In America the number of registrations at the AKC of adult Boxers and litters is falling every year. It is quite common for breeders only to plan a litter when they have a list of new owners waiting for puppies, so you may have to wait six months or more for your puppy, but isn't it worth it? You can share in the anticipation of mating and pregnancy, hear about the puppy soon after birth, visit it two or three times before you take it home. You hope that your new Boxer will be with you for ten, twelve or more years of happy life, so getting it when it is ready, rather than as the instant gratification of a whim is the most sound basis on which to start a lifelong friendship.

Getting a puppy for a birthday present is difficult, for Christmas nearly impossible; the best breeders do not let their pups go into new homes at times of excessive jollity and excitement. Puppy tokens are the thing for presents, a lead or a picture postcard, even a promissory note, then the purchase can be made at leisure. Buying a puppy as a surprise is completely wrong. No reputable breeder sells a surprise which may be more of a shock. The Boxer must be wanted and seen to be wanted, by every member of the household.

Even auxiliary help, such as cleaning ladies and gardeners, should not be against having a big dog around them, as antagonism by anyone can make the dog's life more difficult, and also alter its nature to some extent. We know now that a helper we once had tended to be very rough with the dogs when we were out, driving them indoors with a big stick when they were only puppies. To this day, Naiad has a grudge against men in rubber boots. She now makes the first grab before the kick can start; and Blossom will bare her teeth and growl at anyone carrying a long pole, even on the most harmless business . . . Boxers never forget an injustice, so it is very important to see that everyone co-operates in bringing up your puppy kindly but firmly.

Boxer breeders need a little seeking out. There is a splendid organisation in Britain called Dog Breeders Associates which circulates to prospective owners a list of puppies actually for sale, updated frequently. Breeders must sign an agreement to conform to an ethical code when joining, and they make a small donation for each puppy sold through the organisation. You may also find advertisements for puppies in local papers, and the specialist dog papers, *Dog World* and *Our Dogs* in Britain. You will need to order these from a newsagent as they are seldom on casual sale. The British and American Kennel Clubs will also supply lists of breeders, and the journal of the AKC Pure Bred Dogs carries many advertisements, show wins and notes on the breeds.

In Britain we also have the *Dog Directory,* listing breeders and ancilliary services. This book brings out new editions periodically, and is obtainable from major bookshops. America has a similar publication called *All Breed Pictorial,* listing pedigrees and photographs of individual dogs, with owners' addresses. Veterinary surgeons may be able to tell you of a Boxer breeder locally, and the secretaries of Boxer clubs, listed at the end of the book, will certainly be able to help you. Boxers are scheduled at all the major shows in

USA, Britain and on the Continent, so you may care to start your search by watching dog classes and finding out where the litters are sired by the dog of your choice. Perhaps the most satisfactory way of all is to approach a Boxer owner, and to find out whether he is pleased with his dog and the service he got from the breeder.

In Britain, owners of more than two bitches from which they mean to breed, and sell the pups, are subject to licensing by the local office of the Department of the Environment, whose officers have the freedom to inspect the premises at any time, once licence has been granted. Basic conditions for the licence vary across the country, but in general the inspection is intended to ensure that premises are clean, the animals well kept, well fed, and not a nuisance to their neighbours. Licences under the Breeding of Dogs Act 1974 should state how many breeding bitches may be kept on the premises to avoid over-crowding.

People who hold a breeding licence will be those who breed their bitches regularly, and are knowledgeable about dogs. They may only have three bitches or thirty in a really big kennel. Owners of one or two bitches may breed them without restriction. Quite often such people will only take one litter in the lifetime of each bitch, and the pups you see for sale may be the first litter that person ever reared.

The bigger, long-term kennel gives you the advantage of experience, study of the breed and its peculiar ways, and in such a kennel you may see several generations of related Boxers. On the other hand, it is all too easy for the little kennel to grow until it is almost beyond the labour available, so that the pups' immediate necessities are attended to, but there is too little time left to socialise them. The 'once in a lifetime' litter is a great event in the family's life. Knowledge may be lacking, but there will be great concern and care, and it is likely that the pups will be integrated into the life of the household early, and so very much attuned to humans, and especially to children, a facility very often lacking in the dog from a big kennel. The one litter breeder is not likely to have much advice to offer about your puppy, and will have no facilities to board it for you.

It is felicitous if such a litter is sired by an exhibitor's dog, one you feel is chosen for virtues of temperament or physical conformation. If the sire should be of equally unknown stock, you may suspect that convenience, or neighbourly obligation was the motive. Only you can decide if these two animals will have produced the kind of Boxer you want to own.

The time of year at which you get your pup depends largely on the supply, but other things being equal, I would suggest early Autumn, when holidays are over, the weather is not too bad for house training, and the garden is past its best anyway, so will not be too spoilt by puppy rampaging. It is as well to bear in mind that few boarding kennels will take really young puppies, under six months, so if you have a holiday in view, it will be best to see if the breeder can take the puppy back for that time.

It is useful to get your puppy as near to home as possible, when you may take it back to see the breeder conveniently, and just possibly share the same veterinary surgeon. This can be a great help if any suspected hereditary conditions come up. It is especially pleasant if your puppy can visit the breeder to check that all is well, and perhaps to play with pups of its own age. No other dog plays quite like a Boxer plays, but it is rather sad that because they are rough and boisterous in youth, the single dog seldom gets a work out with a dog of similar weight.

Straight-nosed dogs are often unreasonably frightened of the approach of a Boxer and apprehension is quickly transferred to the owner who will snatch a toy dog up to her bosom, or hustle a larger one away. It is not possible to know why the Boxer is feared by other breeds, but I fancy it may be because of the slightly noisy breathing of the short-faced dog. This noise could be an aggression signal in a longer-nosed dog and is perhaps misinterpreted as such by other breeds.

Within their own household Boxers live happily with other breeds. I have had them with Cavalier King Charles Spaniels, and Bostons, though I did not find Boxer and Great Dane was a compatible combination. They used to spend the day arguing which was the largest at the top of their voices, but this may have been an isolated personality clash, or perhaps it was through boredom, as we had rather too many animals then. I know of one family owning a Rhodesian Ridgeback, Boxer, Basset and Chihuahua very successfully, a Boxer/Bedlington terrier family, Boxer with Siberian Huskies; and lots of Boxers with cats.

A cat supplying the body contact so necessary to the Boxer

Precautions

Before you take your puppy home, you must check garden fences and make them absolutely escape-proof. If the garden is too large for total fencing, make an enclosure in which the puppy can remain, giving you short periods of total peace of mind. This enclosure should have some shade, and a raised bench on which to sit and the puppy may have its toys in here to amuse it. Remember when planning your fencing that Boxers will climb, and also squeeze through small places. It is essential that the puppy is safeguarded from getting away to roads or fields. Make sure that gates cannot be left open, and also have some household drill about opening the front door. The puppy should be shut in another room before the door is opened, otherwise there is every opportunity for it to slip out. So many dogs do this, and are hit by cars, causing distress to everyone concerned.

In both Britain and USA legislation is contemplated to make it an offence to allow a dog to be loose on the road.

Make sure that your dog is covered by third party insurance cover, just in case it trips someone up, or damages livestock or property belonging to someone else. This kind of cover is very inexpensive, but invaluable if the unexpected occurs. Many dog clubs include cover for their members in the membership fee. It is also possible to take out insurance cover, through specialist companies, on the life of the dog, should it die in an accident, and also to cover veterinary fees.

Among other preparations for your puppy, do a check over the kitchen or utility room, where it will spend most of its time while it is young. Electric leads and connections must be well out of the way, as they *have* been bitten through, and families have been cut off the telephone, and gas taps have been turned on; Boxers are so handy with their paws! They soon learn to operate doors which have lever handles, and are adept at getting cupboard doors open.

All poisonous substances should be kept above Boxer height (cleaning fluids are an especial danger) and great care must be taken in the garage not to have pools of anti-freeze on the floor. This deadly poison has a sweet taste which attracts the dog.

Garden poisons need to be banned from the house owning a Boxer puppy, especially metaldehyde slug bait. This is very attractive to the dog and an **instant killer. Weedkiller must be used with the greatest caution; the only** possible time is when the puppy can be excluded from the garden for twenty-four hours. Mouse and rat poison is also attractive to dogs. Warfarin and its derivatives are cumulative poisons which cause internal bleeding and are very dangerous if the puppy gets to a supply several times. If the Boxer has access to even one dose of Warfarin take it to the veterinary surgeon at once for an injection of Vitamin K, the antidote. Household soap once killed a young Boxer. They love soap suds, and will steal a wet cake of soap. This dog attempted to swallow the soap to avoid giving up his prize, and choked in the attempt.

Boxers seem accident prone, and do the most unexpected things. So in owning a Boxer you indeed live dangerously, but life is never dull.

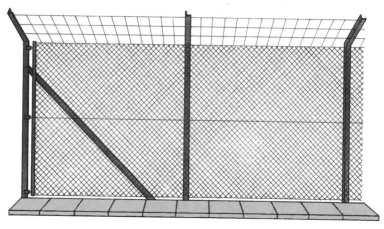

'Boxer-proof' fencing

Interrupted in an escape

Children must learn to be tidy with their toys as plastic ones are most dangerous, and small pieces of plastic can cause an obstruction in the puppy's stomach. Boxers love a piece of cloth to play with (cut the buttons off a garment first), but they should never be given nylon tights. Many veterinary surgeons will recount the emergency operations they have done to remove a length of nylon from a puppy's stomach.

Boxers go wild with excitement over squeaky toys but take care they do not get the squeaker out. They enjoy rawhide chews, and it does not matter if they consume them. Balls must be large enough not to be caught in the throat. An adult can cope with a tennis ball and a partially deflated football gives endless pleasure. They also love a balloon to bounce about on their noses, or a beach ball. The danger lies in too small a ball which may be swallowed. The other great Boxer toy is a specially manufactured rubber grip, to be pulled between two dogs, or dog and owner. Very strong polythene bowls also give a lot of pleasure; they can be carried around like a begging bowl, or worn on the head like a fireman's helmet, or be pushed at great speed across the floor.

Boxers of course, take things they are not supposed to have, and it will always be something you have just handled as it is the owner's scent which attracts them. It will be the *new* book; the gloves you have just been out in; the new possession you have been admiring. They are insatiably curious, always wanting to look at parcels which come into the home, delighting in sniffing over anything new, dribbling on your best suit, and not bothering with your old working clothes. For a non-scenting breed, they learn a lot by their noses, and love to 'read' your trousers when you have spent a day away.

Garden swimming pools are another great puppy hazard; especially when covered with snow and ice as the puppy could fall in and not be able to get out again. Total fearlessness in the breed creates a lot of problems for their owners, so one of the more demanding roles is always to be looking ahead to see what the Boxer might do, and being ready to circumvent it.

The bed for your Boxer puppy is no great problem at first. The best thing is a grocery cardboard carton, with nice high sides, the size which only just fits, as they love the feeling of being supported around their backs. Using such a carton, you will be able to renew it as often as it is chewed, and also get a larger size when the puppy outgrows it. The best bedding will be discarded clothing, (with buttons, buckles, etc. cut off) or old towels. Boxers love to tow their bedclothes about or shred them up, so it is best not to use anything expensive. Later on, the best bed is a home carpentered or made-to-measure wooden bed, on low legs, and with three high sides. In rooms where the dog is supervised, a foam mattress is lovely, and does prevent those ugly callouses which heavy dogs get on hocks and elbows through pressure. On top of this goes a nice blanket. A sheepskin is the utmost luxury for the older dog, but it must be the washable kind.

For puppies that are still destructive, corrugated cardboard makes a good base in their box; for the real demolition worker, a lot of newspaper on top will have to do until better ways are learnt.

If dogs are allowed to sit on settees in the living room, candlewick cotton bedspreads are the most useful form of cover.

Round wicker baskets are always great favourites with dogs, but are not very durable until the dog is quite middle-aged. There are also sag-bags full of polystyrene beads. Very suitable for use in an estate car, greatly loved by dogs, but what a lot of poly beads they hold if just by accident the teeth get through them! When the Boxer is middle-aged and trustworthy, there are lots of nice treats in store which are quite impractical earlier. As the wooden beds are **sometimes heavy to lift, some long trough-type beds made in fibreglass,** bound in metal so they are unchewable are excellent. It is possible to get them with a heating pad built in, and they were invented in this form for the use of the stray dogs in Battersea Dogs Home in London. Ours are completely 'untouched' after a whole year. They have the virtue of being very easy to **clean, and are more hygienic and less chewable than wood, though with a colder surface.**

The very young puppy may be provided with a jacket in the first winter. It must be one that covers the chest, a saddle cloth type is no use at all. The older dog should never need a coat except in illness.

Very old Boxers feel the cold terribly, and will need coats, chest-protecting type, especially for the last run in the garden on winter nights, and even indoors in cold houses. Poppet's favourite is one made of quilted anorak material. Boxer figures are very awkward indeed to fit so it is best to make a **pattern in old sheeting, before cutting into good material. The adult Boxer will**

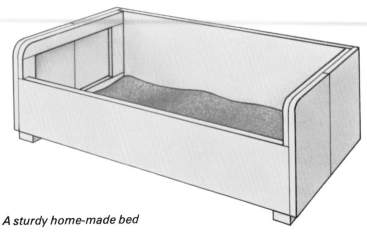

A sturdy home-made bed

normally scorn a coat, and certainly does not need any protection from rain as the hair wipes down easily and will soon dry.

The puppy's first collar should be one with an elastic insert, just in case he gets hung up on a low branch or a cupboard handle. Later we like the rolled leather collars, not wide ones covered in studs which obscure the beautiful lines of the neck. A long lead for training, a short lead for towns, and a nylon slip lead, which incorporates a collar, for exercise walks in the country, complete the Boxer wardrobe, except for the discs bearing your name and address and telephone number, which legally should be worn by every dog outside its owner's premises.

It is important to make provision for putting a temporary or holiday address on the dog. Little cylinders are sold for this purpose, into which a paper can be inserted, but they do come off very easily, so perhaps it is better to buy a special holiday collar, in leather, inside which you can write Holiday Address . . . . The dog is more likely to be lost on holiday than at other times, and if found, application to your home address may be useless at that time.

A fibreglass bed

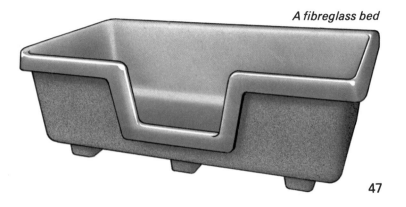

47

*A strong short leather lead with
a secure fastening hook*

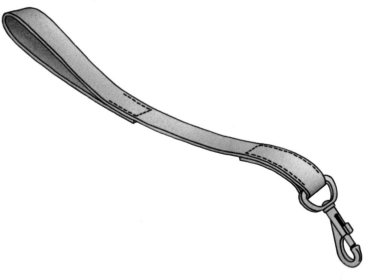

*A coloured nylon slip lead and
collar combined – not safe for town use*

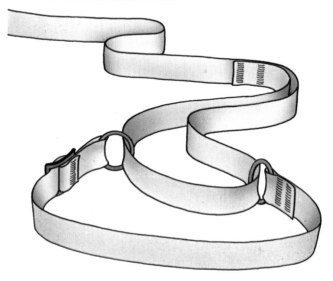

The adult Boxer

In the home

Boxers are a youthful breed, not only in their playful ways which they retain right into old age, but because of their colossal sense of fun. Boxers deliberately make people laugh, well aware that they are acting the clown and this very trait has been the despair of those who have tried to train their Boxer to obedience competition standard.

Breed characteristics are very strong, and every Boxer on our hearth rugs is a Bullenbeisser at heart. They still have the tenacity of purpose, once used to make repeated attacks on the bull, now expressed in a determination to sit next to you on the settee, however much you may forbid it. Tenacity taken to great lengths becomes obstinacy, and the Boxer has that too. Guard instinct develops into a keen sense of possession, which may turn to jealousy. A dominant male will not yield to any adversary, human or animal, without a struggle. Such a dog will always accept a challenge to fight, although the Boxer is seldom the instigator in a scrap between breeds. In short the Boxer is a strong dog with the potential of a killer, which can also be the most tractable of animals, a dog that you can, in truth, trust with your life.

In taking the dog into your home, never lose sight of the need always to be master. The Boxer must always understand that its owner is more powerful than any dog. We reinforce this impression not by physical force, but by endeavouring, when we can, to be just one step ahead of Boxer thinking.

Boxers are dependent on human company to an extraordinary degree, and will almost certainly be destructive if left alone too long. They are almost too intelligent for their own good, as they easily become bored and claustrophobic if shut away. The Boxer puppy will always be a disaster if taken into a home where all the members of the family are away for the major part of each day. Coming in to let the dog out briefly at mid-day is not enough for the Boxer needs company, to be with people, or next best, with other dogs.

When with people, they are quite restful, not busy and continually on the move as terriers and herding breeds are. Boxers are very sensitive to human mood, and also to the age and capacity of the people they are with, one minute lying so quietly on a rug beside a baby, tolerating little fingers in its ears, the next wrestling with no holds barred with teenage boys. The vigilance of the guard dog is turned to close observation of its humans and you will find your Boxer has an uncanny way of knowing what you will do next before the thought is even clear in your own mind.

The Boxer makes the ideal family companion to a group of mixed-aged children, or adults who are active, and not away from the house too long. They really revel in being attached to a hotel, a public house, or some place where there is a lot of action. They do not require a great deal of formal walking exercise, but they like activity in frequent short bouts. Their favourite ploy is to be driven to an open space where they can have about twenty minutes romp, and at other times to have an organised game in the garden. Unless there is very little space available at home, exercising the Boxer need not be a formidable task.

The smooth coat is easy to keep clean, and coat shedding is not a great problem. They do not have a doggie odour, but give off a rather attractive smell of freshly baked biscuit when they are very warm. Great improvement in the breeding of level mouths has largely banished the drooling Boxer, but the blunt nose with nasal secretions caused by excitement can leave trails on house and car windows. The Boxer is not noisy, unless it thinks there are strangers about. They dig a bit in the garden, and they swim if they can. One adult Boxer is an ornament in the garden, two are a tornado going through the herbaceous border.

As a breed they love motoring and they are best in an estate car, where they can lie down. Good ventilation is needed, as the short-nosed breeds always need plenty of oxygen.

I have hardly ever known an irritable Boxer. They are not quick snappers, and in illness are co-operative and cheerful patients for they trust the good intentions of their owners implicitly. Apart from minor digestive troubles, which can usually be dealt with by an adjustment of diet, the companion animal, not used for breeding, keeps very healthy and does not need to see a veterinary surgeon from one annual booster shot to the next.

The Boxer is a loyal and sympathetic companion to the right owner, but may **also be 60lb. (25kg.) of destruction and misery in the hands of a weak** or neglectful owner who is too indolent and lazy to make clear to the dog the limits of acceptable behaviour.

Men like a Boxer, a big dog they are proud to be seen with, a dog which enjoys a wrestle and sparring match. Children like their Boxer because it does amusing things, and will play sensibly as one of a team. Babies learn to walk holding Boxer necks. Women appreciate a Boxer's devotion and guarding ability without unnecessary aggression. The Boxer has a unique sympathy for its owner's moods, and a very special ability to put on a comedy act to jolly its family along. The Boxer can be all things to each member of the community, but they are not an 'everybody's dog', and are not over-effusive with callers until they know them as friends.

Our first Boxer

We saw our first Boxer in 1946; perhaps it would be more accurate to say we half saw her. We were staying in an hotel in Hampshire, and needed to make a trip out to the garage to collect a forgotten bag at bedtime, but in the twilight a dark shape blocked our path. No bark, no growl, just the sound of dragon-like breathing which gave us the message that it would be unwise to move either way. We thought it was a dog, but we had never before seen a dog which behaved with such authority and confidence, and made its intentions so clear without any vocal demonstrations of ferocity.

Suddenly a window opened behind us, and a voice called, 'Right, Zita, let them go!' and the dark shape melted away into the shadows, leaving us free to pass. My husband was deeply impressed with this incident, and in the morning asked to see the guard dog, only to be almost incredulous that the friendly creature, lying on the kitchen floor with toddlers crawling all over her, could be the monster he had feared the night before.

This, he knew, was the dog for him, and so began a love affair which will last to the end of his life. I thought Zita very fine, but not as glamorous as the red cocker spaniel I had set my sights on.

As fate would have it, quite by chance we heard of someone lumbered with the last puppy of a Boxer litter, quite exhausted with all the work it had involved, and anxious to get rid of this bitch for well under the market price.

With some reluctance on my part we went to see the bitch and, of course, she became ours.

Understanding so little about dogs, we expected the new puppy to walk home with us, just because she was of a large breed, although I would have expected to carry a spaniel at the same age. We soon learnt that big puppies are still big babies, and this one was not going to walk anywhere on a lead. We lumped and humped that four-month-old Boxer for about two miles, shifting the saggy burden from one to another. At the end of the journey she had her pet name, Two Ton Tessie.

Inevitably, as I was at home, Tessie was mine all day, by sufferance rather than inclination. Her great big paws thumped about our uncarpeted studio, she was clumsy and mischievous, and already at a gawky, unattractive age. Tessie pulled the spaniels about by their ears and got all the blame for all the dog misdeeds, but she was always cheerful, a totally happy dog. Tessie paved the way for all the Boxer destruction that was to come.

She was the first to be found sitting on a small piece of wickerwork, the shreds of a good dog basket all around her. She was also the first to leap straight through a closed glass door when she was in a hurry to see about intruders in the garden. Tess was teaching us an awful lot about dogs.

There were no distemper vaccines on the market at that time, and dogs were always exposed to the risk of the disease. Tess was infected with the variant of the distemper complex, hard pad, and suffered damage to the central nervous system. During the nursing of her, up to her last days, she was so brave, tractable and tried so hard to co-operate and live, that I too became a Boxer slave, a state which seems now likely to last for ever.

We had bought our own stud dog, a foolish thing to do in many ways, as it can be better to be fancy free to use other people's. On the other hand, the dog you have in your own home can be the only one you know all about, virtues and failings, as we found to our cost when we began to use champion stud dogs which presented a perfect picture in the show ring. It took some time to understand that expert handling can disguise faults of both construction and temperament.

Because of the deadly nature of the virus which killed Tess, we had to wait for another puppy, but we concentrated on finding another descendant of the Palestinian army dog line, a gallant little dark brindle, destined to be mated to Satan, also of War Dog stock. Mating together two dogs of the army strain was a great success.

Families with ex-servicemen fathers flocked to buy them and loved them dearly, but their tradesmen, postmen and neighbours did not fare so well as, although the Boxers were devoted to the immediate family, they regarded all callers as the enemy, so the Boxer owners were virtually imprisoned in their homes.

We had another lesson to learn, that the strong guarding strain in civilian situations can be a liability. We needed to soften up our line with more easy going dogs, and I yearned for a red, as the army dogs were all dark brindles without markings, which reproduced their own colour only. We had no white or check puppies born, and I do not remember hearing that other breeders did. It was only with the fashion for white markings that we got this awful wastage of the white puppies.

In a local market town I saw a bitch being led round the shops, mammary glands dripping with milk, and found she had a well bred litter only two days old. Had I then had the knowledge I have since picked up, I might have concluded that it was quite unnatural for a bitch to be content to leave her litter at that stage, and the warning lights might have indicated that here was some lack of maternal instinct which would not prove the best foundation for a breeding line. Infertility and lack of maternal care was there, strongly hereditary, and we have it with us to this day.

The litter proved ideal for our purpose in other ways, as the bitch belonged to a boy's prep school, so the dam and the litter were well socialised and handled. They were the most people-orientated Boxers I have ever known. Fate was also on our side, as though we chose the plainest bitch, as we did not care for these new fangled white markings, which were just being talked about, we did not get the bitch of our choice. The litter owner telephoned to say that her rich auntie wanted the one we had chosen, so we must take another, one with white markings on the face and white socks. Maybe now we would walk off in a huff, but how glad I am that we were more easily over-ridden in those days, as our 'unchosen' dog turned out to be Pixie, undoubtedly the

The Boxer is superb with children

outstanding dog of our lives and a very great force for the promotion of Boxers among the discerning pet-owning public all over England.

So many people wanted a dog 'just like Pixie' although she never made a competitive appearance in the show ring. Pixie was friendly, clever, amusing, up to all sorts of tricks and yet never a nuisance in public. Always devoted to children through her early conditioning, she did great public service as the leader and patron of the Pixie Club for backward children at a local school. People came to the house especially to enjoy her company. She even had telephone calls made to her. Pixie was very special right up to the end of her eleven and a half years, when she died very suddenly, of heart failure, on our return from a wonderful holiday with her and her daughter Gretel. Sometimes we wonder whether we should blame ourselves for not allowing her to take it easy, not realising that she was becoming an old lady, but her life was so bound up with ours, we think she would have preferred to share everything right up to the end.

It is interesting to speculate why this one bitch had so many good qualities, which we have never managed to reproduce all in one dog again, although many of her descendants echo just some of her ways. She was well-bred, luckily from sound stock, as we did not know enough at the time to question it. She and her dam had a unique opportunity to be conditioned early to people. She came to us as our third Boxer, when we had learnt a little dog psychology, ready for her to teach us more.

Satan and Jill were great companions, a little detached from us and really enjoying kennel life, as their army forbears had done.

From the beginning we were able to consolidate on Pixie's early conditioning, and to make her into a people's dog, sleeping in the bedroom, going out in the car, experiencing everything that human enjoyment had to offer. We were just starting our boarding kennel, so we had many callers for Pixie to meet. In our rambling old farmhouse there was no need to confine her to the kitchen, as there might have been had we been more elegant, or in a built up area, or even if we had more house dogs, as you can't let a crowd of Boxers greet every visitor.

In every way, breeding, socialisation and environment, Pixie had the optimum conditions to develop into a companion dog, and this she did, introducing also something extra which we had not experienced with the army dogs, the bubbling Boxer sense of humour which is such a pleasure to devotees of the breed.

Down the years we kept the army dog strain separate and bred a few of their kind, but the mainstream was the Pixie line, although she was never a devoted mamma, and she and most of her daughters expected me to rear their puppies until they got to the toddler stage, when their dam would begin to enjoy playing with them. This trait made hard work of litter breeding, and from this aspect, we would have been wise to have changed to a more maternal strain.

We very soon felt the effect of Pixie's white markings, as when we mated her to a similarly marked dog, a champion in the show ring where the flashy ones were going to the top, we got our first white puppy, the forerunner of many others which were a heartbreak to destroy. The dark brindle army line went on being 'plain' and never produced whites, even when mated to Pixie's sons who were flashy.

We now have six Boxers as house pets, not an active kennel any more. The oldest is Poppet, aged twelve and a real matriarch, the nominal pack leader, but growing a little tottery on her back legs and gradually relinquishing physical authority in favour of Rooka, great-grand-daughter of Pixie and having some of her charm, though not so sophisticated and urbane, as she has not had the same opportunities for socialisation. Pooka is a disciplinarian who never needs to strike a blow; a hard look and threatening movement of her jaw will quell any upstart dog, family or outsider. She is also very agile, a great play dog, always inviting the others to roll and wrestle, and the only one to be interested in following scent of deer in the forest.

Although Pooka is affectionate, insists on sitting on laps and smothering people with kisses, she very much misses the company of other dogs. She was very melancholy when she and I took a holiday alone whereas another type of character would have revelled in being alone with her owner. Pooka likes it best if her pack and her owners are all at home together. Pooka is our 'talker', a talent some Boxers have to use a special rounded yodelling bark in conversational phrases, which seem to be used as a method of communicating wants and comments.

We have also Pooka's twin daughters, now four years old, by the stud dog Tigger. Having been brought up as one dog, the two are quite indivisible; Naiad the red, and Folly the brindle and white, both answer to each other's names, eat from the same dish, and sleep in a huddle. Folly abandoned her puppies to go out and play with Naiad, and it seems the maternal instinct, never strong in the Pixie line, has almost evaporated altogether, for Naiad proved to be frigid, and refused to allow a dog to mate her, at any stage of her season.

These two devoted sisters are quite unalike in character. Naiad is the very strong guard, persistent and determined, remembering grudges a long time. A sober bitch, given to pacing about like a lioness, on the rare occasions Naiad plays, she likes to crouch in the bushy jungle and spring out on her fellows. Naiad feels the weight of her guarding responsibility keenly.

By contrast, Folly is the fool, soft as a sofa cushion, all wriggles with a rubberface which creases into a grin at the sound of her name. She has almost no guard instinct, accepting all callers as her best friends, but at any excitement she becomes a 'licky' dog, flashing her long tongue all over the windows and doors and people if they come within range. Frau Stockmann mentions she had a bitch with the same habit, but we have not known any others who carry it to quite such lengths. It is possible that licking to excess is an expression of humility as the lower dogs tend to make obeisance and to lick all round Poppet's face, which she objects to as much as we do.

When Folly is frustrated at her attempts to greet people, she retaliates by rushing about panting and dabbling both feet into the water bowl, thoroughly wetting the floor and driving the others to near hysteria by her agitation. Frustration is very strong in Boxers. They can and do wreak their wrath on inanimate objects if they cannot get their own way, especially if they feel guarding is involved.

The twins are affectionate to their owners, but marginally more devoted to each other. This is frequently the case when two puppies are brought up together. Similarly, when Boxers live in a kennel environment they become 'dog's dogs' and not people's dogs.

Our outsider is Blossom. She is of the family but not born here. We bought her at six weeks old, because in shape, colouring, and as it turns out, in temperament, she is a real throwback to the Palestinian army dogs. She has courage, toughness, devotion to owners, but is quite ruthless with those she thinks are up to no good. She also has the traditional Boxer habit of letting strangers in, but not out again. Blossom is a complex character, extraordinarily greedy over food, she would fight the others for the last morsel. She is also very possessive, and if she gets the chance, she will lie across in front of me and order the others to keep away.

If Pooka were not a strong dominator, we should have fights. As it is, Blossom is squashed by strength of will rather than bloodshed, aided by a little judicious separation of the parties when the atmosphere gets tense. Blossom has the genuine physical hardness which has to some extent been lost in the breed. Her coat is longish, a little coarse, but she can endure very low temperatures, remaining outside while the others seek their creature comforts indoors. Blossom could well be, indeed she is a liability and a disturber of the peace. She would probably be better as a single dog in a home, but because her affection is so constantly demonstrated, it seems unfair to send her away. Besides, she will at times show actual defiance of authority, which could lead to her being cruelly treated.

All these five bitches could be described as typical Boxer characters, and they are all completely different, although they share the same environment with no privileges accorded to one in particular, except that Poppet gets the titbits and the softest seat.

The dog Tigger is now five years old; he is a big dog, a strong guard and very suspicious of callers, an athletic animal, jumping over 6ft. (2m.) from a standing postion, though, being heavy, he does not have as much staying power on rambles as the bitches. By nature an undemonstrative dog, he is very quiet and passive in the home, and a restful animal to be with, a great traveller and perfectly behaved, if rather reserved, in public. Owners of rowdy boisterous males would think him a joy to have.

He is certainly easy to deal with, but possibly just a shade boring, maybe because he makes himself subordinate to all the bitches, except when there is need for a mating, when he always reaches target, usually by guile rather than use of his superior weight and strength. Like all Boxer males, he never fights bitches, giving in with a show of indifference over food, or the best sleeping place, but he shows a natural antagonism to any other large male dog.

Of our six resident dogs, Blossom and Naiad would pass the German police dog guard test at any time, and enjoy the opportunity and so would Tigger if we dared to encourage him. Poppet in her youth would also have been excellent. Pooka would probably guard in an extreme situation, but seems to hope she will never be called upon to do so, and Folly fervently believes that a joke and a wriggle will turn evil away. Bearing in mind the close relationship of these Boxers, it is revealing to observe the different types we have, and there are many other variants in character.

All Boxers have a lot in common, but each is different in a way that is not so marked in other breeds. Under a tough trainer who liked to show off a fierce dog, Naiad would be downright dangerous, as she also would be if someone were consistently unjust to her, or physically cruel. Folly would be the despair of formalised training. She could not concentrate sufficiently to learn orders and she again could be the ideal victim for cruelty, as she would find it impossible to believe that the world and all those in it did not exist for good.

Blossom is a one woman dog. She has turned on those who admonished her, even my husband, but her devotion to me is such that one could picture her lying in the snow beside my dying body, were I so misguided as to let that situation arise. Blossom's total devotion was quite unsought on my part as she picked me rather than the other way round. I would rather have Naiad as a special dog, but Naiad prefers her sister . . . the world was ever so.

Blossom now spends much of her time alone with me because she is so naughty that it makes life easier that way. She is a cupboard door opener, a stander-on-hind-legs and reacher, the worst dog in the world, but what is more flattering than being marked down as a dog's most treasured possession . . . . and Blossom chose me.

The one man dog is unusual in the Boxer breed; they are more frequently deeply attached to all members of the household in which they live, with, in addition, a short list of close friends.

The adaptable Boxer – guardian, athlete, clown and playmate

Dog and bitch

Boxer males, especially those used at stud, have a difficult youth. At around twelve months, the male is a weighty, boisterous, exhuberant animal whóse enthusiasms are difficult to subdue. Ideally the dog should meet all visitors and be conditioned to quiet behaviour, but many of us have to take the line of least resistance and shut the young Boxer away when guests come, so that the dog may become suspicious of all callers, or extremely anxious to get at them, not learning a balanced demeanour until middle age.

In adolescence, the male hormones are often out of balance for a while, and the dog will have more exaggerated sexual impulses than will be apparent when it has settled to adulthood. Exhibition of sexual tendencies at this time do not mean that the dog should be put to a bitch. In fact it is much better if the companion dog is never used at stud at all. To allow one stud episode to oblige a friend, or even to get a pup of his to keep, is to some extent cruel, as it will make the dog more aware of bitches, more inclined to fight, and to escape to follow bitch scent. The male that has never been used at stud does not miss what he has never known.

Many owners are anxious to see their dog achieve adult status by raising its leg to urinate. This usually happens, with a bit of trial and error, at around one year old, but has no significance if it takes longer. Males need to mark their territory, by directing a stream of urine at special marking posts, sometimes shrubs and plants in the garden. Douse them quickly with a bucket of water as otherwise they will wither for sure! Territory has to be re-marked if another male, or a bitch in season has visited, or passed the fence. In such cases the dog may 'mark' inside the house, against furniture and curtains, much to your displeasure, which you must certainly express to him. But blame yourself also, for you should have foreseen that this might be done as it is a natural canine impulse. In breeders' households, and commercial kennels, where there are many visiting bitches, it is not practical to allow the males into the house at all.

The male dog will often have one drop of yellowish coloured exudate at the tip of the penis; this is a natural secretion which the dog will clean from time to time, and need not worry the owner. Male Boxers are not so possessive about their owners. They are cool and more detached in their attitude, while still remaining affectionate. Bitches love their owners passionately, and ask nothing better than to be beside them. Damage and destruction is usually aimed at getting out to be with their owner.

If you decide you would like to own both a dog and a bitch, or to supplement your male with a slightly easier female, you will have to make up your mind that one or the other will have to be neutered, or else one, most likely the bitch, will have to be boarded during her seasons. It is quite impossible to keep a male dog from a bitch in the acute phase of her heat in the normal household. Indeed, it can be very cruel to the dog to have an interesting bitch so near; they usually lose a lot of weight and condition through expending nervous energy at this time, and they will perform some astonishing feats of escapism to get at each other.

You can have a vasectomy performed on the dog. This will not curb its mating urges at all, but will ensure that it does not father any puppies. You may well feel, as I do, that this half way stage is of little use. The dog may be neutered through castration. Many people, including most vets, have more reservations on this than they have on hysterectomy for the female. The testicles are removed, leaving the scrotal sac. In a dog that is difficult to manage, given to escaping, or too volatile, the temperament will mellow after castration, but the improvement takes some time to become apparent. There may be alteration in the coat texture, or baldness, and a tendency for weight to accumulate. Castration of the male dog should not take place until it is mature, and is an operation performed by the veterinary surgeon under general anaesthetic. Patients do not generally interfere with their stitches, although they must be exercised on the lead until they are completely healed.

It is possible for a vet to give a hormonal injection which will mimic the action of total castration, the effect lasting about 10 days so you may see if the difference is going to be as you wish.

A castrated dog has no desire to mate bitches, and does not feel the urge for ritual marking.

The bitch should be in oestrus (on heat or come into season) for the first time at about eight months of age, a little later than some breeds, repeating the season at six monthly intervals, counting from the first day of the last season. That is the textbook formula, but few bitches keep to it; a first season at ten months, or any time up to two years is not really abnormal, but a late start does seem an indication of infertility. Naiad and Folly were 18 months before their first season, so then I got the warning bells about their lack of fecundity. Although freedom from oestrus may seem a useful bonus in the companion bitch, it can mean some abnormality of the reproductive organs which will give trouble later, so veterinary advice should be sought.

Many bitches have intervals of eight months between seasons and this would seem so common as to be normal. The Boxer bitch is unfortunate in making a lot of mess when she is in season, as there is no coat as protection. A lot of blood-stained discharge will be dropped as she moves about, and more will be found on her bed. The lack of camouflaging coat makes it very obvious when she is 'coming in' as the vulva swells to great size. The bitch is attractive to dogs before the blood-stained discharge appears, but at this time, and for the suceeding eight or nine days, she will not allow a male to approach, but it is not possible to take her out in public, as dogs will pester her with their attentions.

Bitches kept together may simulate mating action. This is a normal behaviour and should not be stopped, unless it is very irritating to the other bitch. The bitch is vulnerable to mating from the ninth to the fifteenth day of her season, and she will do her utmost to meet with the opposite sex, so extreme vigilance is necessary. After the fifteenth day, dogs will still be interested, but the bitch is likely to repulse them. Optimum mating days vary very much with individuals, so it is important to keep tight control until the vulva has shrunk again, and the discharge, which pales to white around the eleventh day, has totally ceased.

Many Boxer bitches suffer really deeply from phantom or false pregnancies, mimicking in every detail a bitch that has been successfully mated. The actual

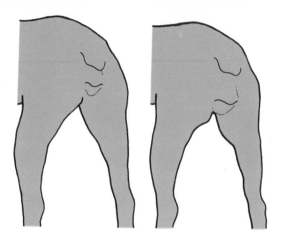

Left: normal rear view of bitch and right: swollen vulva of the bitch at peak oestrus (ready for mating)

performance is incredibly like the real whelping, with abdominal enlargement, milk in the mammary glands, the bitch seeking seclusion and possessive behaviour with small objects as surrogate puppies. If you are not aware of this phenomenon, you may be really worried, like the owner who telephoned to say she thought her bitch had gone mad, she had taken to her basket, growling, and guarding two plastic pepper pots. Frustrated bitches which live in kennels will willingly suckle orphan puppies, or even make an older pup, or a kitten submit to being babied. You will find that these mock symptoms of whelping come at just the right date, ten and a half weeks after the start of the last season.

Your veterinary surgeon can help you by drying off the milk and giving tablets to alter the hormonal acitivity, although in mild cases giving less food and liquid, and providing more exercise help to take the bitch's mind off her sad state. It is a great mistake to let her become fanatical about her invisible puppies. She may become temporarily snappy with children, and work herself into an uncomfortable state by over–producing milk. The best treatment is 'come for a walk and forget it'.

If a bitch has phantoms after every season, it is best to have her spayed, a total ovario-hysterectomy, removing both uterus and ovaries. It is a complete misconception to think that having a litter will cure the tendency to phantom pregnancies.

If you have no intention of breeding from your bitch, there is a very good case indeed for having her spayed, provided that she has had at least one full season and is near to two years old. To have the operation done too early leaves the bitch physically and mentally immature, with a tendency to be dull. Bitches do not automatically put on weight after spaying as people fear. Their weight and activity depends entirely on the amount of stimulus offered. The spayed bitch has the advantage of always being available to accompany the family, and she does not suffer the ignominious banishment to the kitchen which the bitch in full oestrus must endure, unless you put her into panties, a thing I have never been able to tolerate, although many owners find the idea useful, if it does not offend them aesthetically.

Spaying is a major operation, involving some element of risk to life, but this is very small now that small animal surgery has improved so much, and modern anaesthetic apparatus is available. Many vets keep the bitches overnight, but if the operation is done in the morning, it is possible to take the bitch home, provided she is nursed carefully. She should be almost back to normal next day. No dressings are put on the operation wound, which in the Boxer will be from choice down the mid-line of the abdomen, as the flank, the alternative site, scars so badly in the Boxer. The stitches are seldom any worry to the bitch and they are removed about the tenth day after the operation.

Work by researchers in USA has revealed that bitches spayed after their first season are less likely to have mammary cancers than bitches which continue to have regular oestrus cycles but are not bred from.

A more temporary method of contraception is by means of injection or oral treatment with the 'pill', compounds of megestrol acetate. Correct use of these preparations, available under different brand names in all countries, will postpone or prevent oestrus, reduce sexual urges, and treat false pregnancy, but as the uterus of the bitch is very sensitive to alteration in hormone balance, timing of the dose, and the amount administered need careful consideration.

It is not uncommon for Boxer bitches to show all the signs of pro-oestrus, with vulva swelling and some excitement, but hormone levels lag behind, and oestrus proper does not take place, frequently until eight weeks later. There is probably a familial tendency to this behaviour. In this case, if the 'pill' course is started too early, the whole system may be confused and subsequent heats will be speeded up; this factor has led to some veterinary surgeons having suspicions about the usefulness of this type of contraception. The onus for correct timing lies with the owner, who can give with absolute accuracy a history of the bitch's oestrus cycle. It is well established that bitches kept together will induce each other to come into season. Experimental bitches have been given the 'pill' for nine consecutive seasons with no ill effect, and have subsequently been successfully bred from, but dosage and timing are crucial in making it effective for the pet bitch. If you wish to use this method it is important to talk it over with your veterinary surgeon well ahead of time. The cost is considerably less than the charge would be for boarding a Boxer bitch for three weeks.

The bitch which gets accidentally mismated can be aborted within 36 hours of the mating, the sooner the better. Abortion is not possible later than this. The abortion will be brought about by an injection of stilboestrol, which may have the effect of bringing the bitch into season for another three weeks or longer, and also may cause severe changes in the uterus, making breeding impossible later, or opening the way to uterine disease. You will find your veterinary surgeon may refuse to abort the bitch in this way more than once. If at all possible, the pregnancy should be allowed to continue and the puppies reduced down to two in number, just enough to take care of the milk supply.

Boarding and travelling

Many general boarding kennels will take any breed . . . except the Boxer. They are notoriously bad at doing what they do not want to do, being where they have no wish to be. If the Boxer is determined to pine, it will do so despite all the kennel owner can do for it. In spite of being well fed it will lose weight, and the general despondency may trigger off some other illness which was latent. You may come back to a very sad Boxer indeed, and it will not necessarily be the kennel people's fault.

The other type of reaction is to be determined to get out, to tear at wire with unbelievable strength, or to jump impossible heights. Such Boxers can do themselves an injury; again, no one's fault but its own. The urge to get out is not usually to run away but much more likely a desire to be inside the house. Many a boarded Boxer has ended up having full house privileges and the kennel owner's dogs have taken its place in the compound. The damage a Boxer can do to kennelling is considerable, so it is easy to see why they are not the most welcome of guests.

If you visualise the need to board your Boxer frequently, begin when it is quite young, six months to a year, and take it somewhere where they understand and like Boxers. It is best to inspect kennels and look at facilities during the Spring and Autumn, before the boarding season is at its height. If it is at all possible, go where there are Boxers bred, for a dog will often delight in having the chance to play with its own kind, or to share a kennel with one of the opposite sex. It is all a matter of early conditioning.

Nearly all Boxers are good travellers and very much enjoying motoring. For the exception, just go on taking it in the car, on an empty stomach, and in the end, the drooling and sickness will stop. This is much better than giving travel sickness tablets, which are all in some degree tranquillisers, and make the dog dopy, unsteady on the feet and not really enjoying the outing.

A peculiarity of some Boxer bitches is that they will not urinate when away from home, or away from the same type of ground. If they are used to grass, then you may search in vain at a rocky-based seaside town for a suitable spot. We once had a bitch hold up for forty-eight hours because she was not suited, and the situation was only resolved when she fell off the boat into the sea so having no choice. Urination to the bitch seems to confer some degree of honour to the place and the people around; we always felt glad when a boarder had done its first puddle. The male sex is never any problem in this way; if they hold up urination at all, it is due to nervous tension.

Fighting

As a consequence of their devotion and guard instinct, Boxers quite enjoy a fight, to the death if necessary, re-awakening the old battling spirit of the bull-baiters. Poppet, now such a respected old lady, was one of the worst fighters, and still bears the scars of the many repair jobs the vet did on her.

Boxer vendettas last for months and years, always simmering but at times maintaining a veneer of toleration and friendship, while looking for the right opportunity to fight again. If a Boxer male takes a dislike to a neighbour's dog, as may well happen if the Boxer did not initiate the first fight, you can never really be happy about the two meeting again.

In a Boxer kennel, once the two enemies have started, the rest of the pack will join in, fighting each other quite without discrimination for the pure joy of the battle. Noisy fights with roaring are much less severe than the silent variety. There are almost never squeals of pain. The Boxer takes injury in such circumstances stoically, but will scream if you tread on its toe or pull an ear by accident.

We find that mothers and daughters never fight, nor does dog with bitch, but other relationships can have a flare up, and the Boxer will not tolerate another dog being introduced into the household without a lot of preparation. Many people are hesitant about keeping two males together; there is nearly always a fight over precedence, particularly if there is the scent of a bitch on the air.

Fights are always sudden, with no growling as warning, but sometimes you will catch the challenging glare which is the customary prelude to attack. Stopping a fight is a matter of improvisation at the time. Anything and everything has worked for us, but seconds never seem so long as when you are trying to break a fight up and are having no success at all. Twisting collars to cut off the air supply works, or a spray of cold water from the garden hose: a sudden crashing noise, like throwing the bucket against a wall, or ringing the door bell, may distract the fighters and just give you time to separate them behind strong doors. If you do not part them quickly, they will be into the fray again.

If a group is fighting, remove the less engaged ones first, leaving the main protagonists till last. You have not much choice anyway. Screaming, shouting, and hitting either of the dogs is no help. Their ancestry has conditioned them to shutting out all pain while they are fighting. Once again, you have to be more clever than they are, not stronger. Once the fight is over, Boxer bitches will show each other great sympathy, and spend hours licking the wounds they caused each other.

If your Boxer should be attacked while on the lead, do not drag the dog back in such a way that its forelegs are off the ground, as the adversary can inflict terrible injuries to the abdomen which would not normally be exposed in a 'free' fight. The dog's natural instinct is to fight low and close to the ground, taking the injuries on legs and neck. The average companion Boxer does not pick a fight but is not slow to accept a challenge.

If a small dog insults a Boxer, the instant action will be to pin the small dog to the ground, under the Boxer's chest, and hold it there without doing physical harm. Judicious action will enable you to get the Boxer off without further injury to the other dog, but only if the other owner will be sensible and stand away. Screaming, pulling and endeavouring to rescue a little darling may result in biting which would not take place in more rational handlings.

General care

Feeding

The Boxer is not normally a greedy dog; only Blossom puts her stomach before any other interest, and we can count on one hand the number we have had with this tendency over all our dog-years. The Boxer digestive system is very sensitive, and closely linked to the emotions. If there are strangers in the house, the dogs will not eat until they have gone away. They seem unwilling to concentrate on food while their minds are disturbed.

Extreme leanness is not at all uncommon in the adolescent Boxer. They can be well muscled and very fit but with not an ounce of fat to spare, if they have a lot of exercise or reason to expend their nervous energy. A bitch in season, or decorators in the home can take pounds off the Boxer, and they will not eat larger meals to regain the weight. Some Boxers are really good eaters and need to be strictly rationed with food, but you should consider yourself lucky if you get one of this type. It will probably be more placid and self-assured generally. Many Boxers do not succeed in looking well covered until they are around four years old. Naiad and Folly have only just achieved it, having looked like animated anatomical diagrams since late puppyhood. Their appearance should now stabilise, until they go into old age at around ten years, when appetite flags again, but in the elderly dog it is more 'can't be bothered to eat' than 'too busy to eat', as in the young dog.

Many Boxers suffer from periodic indigestion, evidenced by refusal of food, tympany in the gut, (really loud tummy noises which can be heard all over the room), but there is no sign of actual pain. The dog will usually eat grass, in order to vomit, sometimes getting so desperate as to eat some other substance as an irritant if they cannot get to grass. Newspaper, carpet or house plants have all been devastated during a dyspeptic bout. The grass or its substitute is usually vomited quite quickly, surrounded with white froth and a tinge of yellow bile.

Food refusal usually goes on for twenty-four hours. Sometimes the cause of the upset may be traced to over-rich food with a high fat content. Naiad and Folly stole four packets of margarine, and ate the lot, containers and all. They were very sick, but not sorry. Boxers vomit easily and will, if allowed, eat the offending substance again immediately. We once had a bitch which regularly ate her food and almost immediately vomited it back, so that she could enjoy it again. We never found any explanation, other than that she ate too quickly the first time.

Apart from over-rich food, meat with too much fat, and blood-soaked meats like heart, the other explanation for the Boxer's tendency to dyspepsia and flatulence is that they swallow a great deal of air as they gulp down their food. The formation of their mouth does not allow the dainty nibble which a sharp-nosed dog uses. Dogs do not chew their food, so digestion begins in the stomach. Large-headed breeds should not be given anything in big lumps, as these are liable to be vomited back at best, or at worst to cause an obstruction and choking.

Another digestive disability is a breed tendency to malfunction of the exit valve from the stomach, the pyloris, allowing food to be vomited in undigested state twelve hours or more after it has been taken, and leading in extreme cases to the very dangerous condition of bloat. Boxer feeding therefore requires great care, regularity, and very little variation in menu.

As the Boxer has this slightly delicate digestion it is better to avoid the highly palatable, spiced tinned dog foods which can give rise to the production of very obnoxious gas, especially noticeable when voided while sitting around the fire on a winter evening. If this gas is a real nuisance, it may be curbed by a plain diet, more exercise, and antibiotics from the veterinary surgeon to control bacterial action.

There are two important facts to establish about Boxer feeding. The first is that the dog does not require an all-meat, or especially high protein diet, and the second is that variety, in line with the human menu, is a positive disadvantage. Once you have found a meal formula which suits your dog, I advise keeping to it, week in and week out, only making changes if really necessary, over a period of three weeks, adding a little of the new food each day. Many owners worry about what the dog would eat 'in the wild' and try to reproduce such a diet, but in Boxers we have a man-made breed which was never wild, and even if its ancestors were, many thousands of years of adaptation have taken place since then.

The Boxer needs a balanced diet, containing carbohydrates, protein, fat, vitamins, minerals and water. There are many ways to provide such a diet now, ranging from the most expensive and time consuming, involving raw meat of the quality passed for human consumption, through to commercially produced complete diets which are fed straight from the sack, except for the need to soak in cold water. These diets are certainly time saving, and may be cheaper when the cost of fresh meat fluctuates. Really cheap feeding, of meat scraps, brawns or unbranded tinned meat, does not suit the Boxer at all. Unfortunately, they can never be inexpensive dogs to keep, but they do not need unnecessary luxury either.

Undoubtedly, the Boxer will prefer fresh meat. It is all too easy to get addicted to it, and then you have a dog which will eat nothing else, but this regime is expensive and also subject to criticism by others who contend that animals should not deplete the world's store of protein available for human consumption.

The formula for feeding fresh meat will be: for every 8oz. (250g.) beef, lamb, rabbit or chicken, add 8oz. (250g.) wholemeal broken biscuit meal, or stale brown bread; 1 drop of fresh codliver oil; ½ teaspoonful of sterilised bone flour.

This is the ratio of carbohydrate to protein and fat, vitamins and minerals. The young adolescent male, at the peak of his growth, may require a daily ration of two pounds of meat, and two pounds of kibbled meal, plus proportionate codliver oil and bone flour. This will be broken down into two or three feeds, as suits him best. It is impossible to be precise on quantity of feeding, as it varies so much with the individual, the amount of mental stress and physical activity, and the way these factors affect your dog.

While the Boxer is growing, up to two or two and a half years, you will aim to feed enough to satisfy appetite and promote growth, also providing, if possible, enough to give the dog a slight covering of fat over the muscles of shoulders and hindquarters. The dog putting on too much weight early, the good food converter, must be restricted, but no attempt must be made either to stunt or promote growth by cramming with food. Fatness is always to be avoided in the Boxer.

In the puppy it is not wise to put too much weight on developing bones and joints, and in the adult dog obesity restricts activity and puts undue strain on the breathing mechanism and the heart. In the adult, diet should be regulated to keep weight level, especially in the spayed bitch which is relieved of the stresses of hormonal swings.

If the Boxer is frequently on the receiving end of biscuits from children, or nuts and crisps at parties, then the carbohydrate content of its regular meals should be cut to compensate. Ideally, dogs will not be given titbits, but the fascination of sharing with the dog is great, and makes it seem more like one of the family.

The cheaper version of the fresh meat diet is to use meat which has been passed for animal consumption only, bought from specialist shops and usually marked with a green or purple dye. This meat will be unfit for human consumption in some way, and there is always the likelihood that these could be the carcases of sick animals which have been extensively treated with drugs which have not been excreted before death. The abattoirs from which such meat comes do not pretend to reach a high standard of hygiene, so this meat should not be kept in the household refrigerator. It must be cooked, and all boards and knives used for meat preparation should be boiled after use. The same precautions apply to washed and unwashed tripes for animal consumption . . . Boxers rarely like the tripe sold for human use.

The carbohydrate portion of the food can be biscuit meal, in the smallest grade, which must be pre-soaked for about one hour, in hot water, before being fed. The liquor in which a chicken carcase has been boiled is also good, but salted meat extracts are not liked, and should not be used, especially for puppies.

The best biscuit meal for the Boxer is an absolutely plain one. Cereal foods containing a loose mixture of flaked maize do not suit at all, as they blow the loose flakes out of their bowls and across the floor, and the maize comes through the intestine totally undigested. It may be argued that it provides roughage, but my dogs keep equally well on a low residue food. Brown bread is very much liked, but mouldy bread should not be used, as there is the rare chance that one of the moulds might be toxic.

When using fresh meats, raw or cooked, vitamins and minerals will need to be added, but the amounts should be very carefully measured and balanced, particularly with regard to the fish liver oils, containing Vitamins A and D which, if given in excess, cause as much bone disease as when there is deficiency. The easiest way for most owners is to use a complete mineral and vitamin preparation formulated for dogs, and to follow the instructions for the weight of the dog accurately. Do not give any halibut or codliver oil in addition.

If you wish to supply the Vitamins in their natural form, then the amount of codliver oil, proportionate to the formula, must be given accurately, and bought in small quantities as it deteriorates quickly. B group vitamins will be contained in the biscuit meal and the bread, and the dog does not need Vitamin C, as it makes it own within the body if allowed access to adequate sunlight, as any pet Boxer will be.

The most important mineral for the dog is calcium phosphate and this is best supplied in the form of steamed bone flour. Salt may also be added to the amount of 1% of the dry weight of the dog's dinner, although if bread is being used, it will contain an element of salt. Vitamins and minerals are important to the growing animal and the pregnant bitch. Otherwise the dog will do well enough without expensive additives, especially if cooked liver is fed in small amounts once a week. Liver can be addictive, and is also laxative in quantity, so keep it a once a week treat.

Many owners find that tinned dog meats are palatable and also convenient to feed, but do read the labels, and take account of the amount of meat, cereal and water that the tin contains. You may not be feeding as well as you think you are. Some of the cheaper varieties are intended to be fed as complete diets, as they contain a lot of cereal, so you will need to buy more tins, and you may be overloading your dog with carbohydrate and making it fat, at the expense of body building growth. Many tinned dog foods contain all the vitamins and minerals necessary, so you will not have to buy any additives of that kind.

There are available in Britain blocks of deep frozen dog food, consisting of tripes with cereal, pre-cooked. Boxers like this very much and do well on it, the disadvantage being the need for slow defrosting, and the disagreeable smell, both of the product and the dog which has eaten it. They seem to exude these strong smells through the skin, as well as on the breath.

The most modern form of feeding is by expanded meals containing balanced cereal, fat and protein, vitamins and minerals in pellet form. For the Boxer these meals must be soaked in *cold* water, as if soaked in hot the fat will make them become sticky. Boxers do very well on complete diets with only fresh cold water in addition.

The amount of fat the diet contains is the guide to palatibility, one containing a high proportion of fat (24%) is readily eaten on its own while other complete diets may need the addition of a little tinned meat, or cheese, just the smallest amount to make it tasty and to supply the variety which some owners feel they must give their dog to bring it more in line with the family's meals. For one Boxer, scraps from the family table would be an excellent addition to a complete dog diet. It would be extravagant and wasteful to add significant amounts of specially bought protein.

We use a complete diet high in fat content, imported from America. Surprisingly, although the Boxer is usually intolerant of fat it seems easier to digest when incorporated into a complete diet, and in this form does wonders for the coat, leaving it shiny and gleaming with hardly any grooming. We add nothing to this diet, beyond soaking in cold water, so it is quick and easy to feed, but not cheap. The version for dogs under maximum stress, with the

Rewards are appreciated

highest fat content, was the only food to put a becoming layer of fat on Naiad and Folly, and also on Tigger when he was in an anxious mood about bitches. We stop using this grade of food directly improvement is seen, usually in two to four weeks.

The Science formulated diet we are using at present is very low residue, **giving obvious advantages and no drawbacks that we can see after a whole** year of use. Some of the complete diets make dogs produce large volumes of bulky stools, especially when first changing from meat and cereal diet.

Among other foods worth considering are well boned fish, and hardboiled eggs, and cheese. Raw herrings and raw eggs are not to be given, as they contain an element which destroys other vitamins. Though it must be said that many a Boxer has stolen half a dozen eggs and come to no harm, to feed them regularly would be asking for trouble. Milk is of doubtful value after puppy days. Some dogs cannot digest the lactose in milk, and most find it laxative. The milky foods are usually the ones the puppy first discards when it comes off its four meals a day routine.

Many Boxers love soft fruit and will strip raspberry canes and bramble bushes. They also like to share in oranges, apples and bananas. Share is the important word; the Boxer loves to be included in what the family has, and especially to be bought its own ice-cream cornet like the other children.

We give our Boxers a few hard biscuits in the mornings, and as hello and goodbye treats . . . (Boxers soon get you into these routines). We use only the small biscuits, as hoarding can cause jealousy where there are other animals.

Grinding on a bone helps puppy teeth fall out, making way for the adult set at

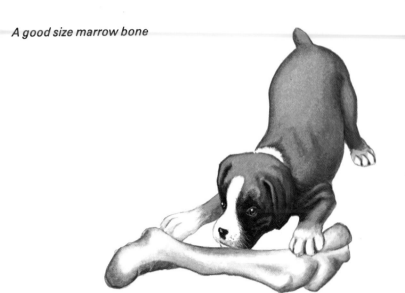

about four months. A really large marrow bone, left unchopped, is the only type permissible. After four months, no bones at all as Boxer jaws are so powerful it is easy for them to get splinters off and to cause an acute abdominal emergency. Our vet says he has seen so many that he would unconditionally ban the bone. Boxers eat a lot of grass, not only as an emetic, but they actually graze and enjoy it, especially the new young lush growth.

In illness when a light diet is required, it is usual to give plain boiled rice, and small amounts of chicken or white fish, or lean lamb, in very tiny quantities six times a day until the dog is tolerating food well, and not vomiting. In even more extreme illness, with high fever, try a jelly made from pulverised chicken or beef.

On recovery from illness, a baked egg custard is always appreciated, so are sardines, (drained of oil), roast chicken, warm from the oven, Stilton cheese, or any other strong smelling variety, and marmalade on buttered toast.

Fresh water must always be available to the dog. It must be changed frequently, and never left outside all night, in case it is contaminated by rats or other livestock. Ice is appreciated in the bowl in summer, or ice cubes given to lick. The water bowl must be washed frequently, to clear the residue of saliva the Boxer deposits in it. Feeding bowls are expensive in polished metal, but are undoubtedly the most durable, as enamel chips dangerously, and plastic will be chewed round the edges and no longer hygienic.

The water bowl should be heavy, as some Boxers will carry it about in order to raise a laugh; some, like Folly, wash their feet in it; most Boxers take a drink and dribble the residue on your skirt; it's all part of life with the Boxer.

Feeding bowls in polished metal are the most durable

Training

Training your Boxer starts as soon as you leave the breeder's home with your puppy, for someone is going to hold the puppy still in their arms in the car, restraining its efforts to struggle, and using their voice to calm its fears. Training means not only having your dog obey orders, it also involves forging a relationship of mutual trust so that your dog is more likely to do as you want, or rather *not do* as you don't want. Training the Boxer is best done by prevention rather than cure. The owner takes care not to let bad behaviour happen so that doing the right thing becomes a habit.

Housetraining is more a matter of training the owner to watch the puppy, to take it outside directly the warning signals are given, and to stay with it all the time until results are obtained, and then to lavish on the praise. The staying outside is the worst part, for puppy minds are easily distracted, and when you have rushed your pup outside, when it was just on the point of urinating, you may then conclude that nothing was further from its mind, as it begins to chase a leaf, or look up at the sky in wonderment. If you decide that perhaps you were mistaken, and take the pup back in ... then, on the carpet! Mistakes that happen indoors are due to lack of vigilance on the part of the owner, or lack of patience in staying with it. Just putting the pup out and shutting the door on it teaches nothing at all. You need to take it to the same site in the garden, for associated smells, and you should also use encouraging words, a phrase of your own choice, but always the same one.

Puppies pass urine on waking from sleep, sometimes during play, and they always defecate straight after eating. You will soon come to interpret correctly the anxious look which comes with the desire to evacuate. Boxers are very easy to housetrain, provided you do your part. If you are too preoccupied to notice the pup's intention, it cannot at this stage wait for you, and a puppy shut in a room alone cannot be blamed for what it does.

Activity and nervous strain increase the gut motility and the urge to empty the bladder, so you will get more mess from the stressed puppy left alone than you would in normal circumstances. Smacking the pup when you find a pool does no good at all, unless you actually catch it in the act of making it, and opportunity to be clean outside has been recently given. Old-fashioned hate-demonstration, like rubbing noses in excreta, degrades both you and the dog and teaches nothing; just as it would not do to a child. You may, if you think it just, admonish with your voice, and a sensitive puppy will feel disgrace and shame, sometimes demonstrated so abjectly that you will be forced to make up the quarrel. Boxers are very good at letting anger evaporate. Early housetraining by the use of 'magic' words is very useful all through life. It can be convenient in a show dog, or any dog which you take about with you, to tell it to go and urinate and have it do so on command. We say, 'Go and be good', and they do . . . even making the action if they don't really want to.

In my experience, neither puppy nor adult Boxers bark to go outside to be clean. They walk about looking worried, or they stare at the door, or sit with noses close to the opening. They expect you to be watching them, as they spend so long watching you. Adult dogs and bitches can hold urine for very long periods, but if forced to break housetraining because of some default of their humans, no mention should be made of the mistake as the dog will feel shame enough anyway. Bitches coming into season often urinate far more frequently than usual, probably because of heightened excitement.

Boxers particularly appreciate closeness and being touched. They lie close together, piled upon one another, and with people, they love to be in contact. You will find your puppy sits on your feet while you are working in the kitchen; Blossom lies on my heels while I am weeding the garden, they love to huddle and cuddle, so keep them as clean and attractive as possible, so that you like to have your dog near you.

Another big hurdle is to choose and teach the pup its name. I always pick the puppy up and say its name slowly right into its face. Whether it helps or not I do not know, but it pleases me, and that is largely what puppy owning is about. The name, short and crisp, should be used on every occasion you address the puppy. You will find the puppy wants to come to you, so use the name as it comes, when you pick it up, when you feed it. Two or three days will have its name firmly fixed in its mind. Most adult Boxers respond to two or three variations of their name, among other words. We once counted how many words Pixie knew, and I think it amounted to over thirty, which she could accurately interpret. It never fails to astonish me that my crowd know each other's names, and always identify the one called. If I am calling Pooka, the others will turn their heads in her direction. Names are very important to dogs, they love to hear them, and will respond to their name when used in ordinary conversation, so pick a nice one.

The next word to teach is 'no!' a word most frequently in use from now on, always prefaced by the puppy's name. But do be generous with the 'good boy' or 'good girl' too as praise goes such a long way with Boxers. They love to feel they have pleased you.

The puppy must not go outside your garden, unless carried, until after it has had its full course of preventative inoculations against distemper, hardpad and infectious jaundice, and also against rabies in those countries where the disease is indigenous. The timing of the course, and the length of time before the pup is protected depends very much on the brand of vaccine used, which will be decided by your veterinary surgeon. It is as well to make arrangements for the vaccination programme directly you know when you will collect your puppy. The litter will have been protected for a certain length of time, by antibodies from the dam via the first milk, but this natural immunity wanes at between four and twelve weeks. As distemper vaccine is a live virus, it is important that your pup is absolutely free from concurrent infection when it goes for vaccination.

If you take the puppy to the vet's surgery, it must be carried and left in the car until the vet is ready for it. Do not risk picking up an infection in the surgery from another patient. Sometimes a pup will show reaction at seven to ten days after the first distemper injection, when it will be just a little quiet and depressed for one day. This is a sign that antibodies are forming, and is no cause for worry, provided the pup is back to normal within twenty-four hours.

For the first few nights that the Boxer puppy is in your home, I suggest that it should sleep in the bedroom in a box beside someone's bed. This companionship at night need not last more than one or two weeks, but I am sure that it pays dividends, both in continuing housetraining and because it eliminates loneliness and claustrophobia during the transition period from being part of a litter, to being a self-contained dog.

Consider what will happen if you shut the puppy alone in the kitchen at bedtime. It may sleep for a short while, and then it will wake and start to call for its dam and fellows, as is only natural in a pack animal. Perhaps you go and reassure the pup, and then it calls again, and you go again, and you also stay to wipe up the puddles it will have made while it was wakeful. The little Boxer soon discovers that it can get company by screaming for you, so it goes on to do so, tyrannising the whole household. Perhaps you will soon have had enough of this, and will administer a slap and a sharp word, which will seem very odd behaviour indeed to the pup, when he has had nothing but loving attention from you all day. Why switch it all off suddenly after dark? This is treatment which it has never experienced before, and the automatic response in the dog is either to look very warily at you, not knowing whether it will get a slap or a welcome (after all, night and day were not very different to the pups in the nest) or you will lay the foundation of a dog which is always nervous about staying alone.

To achieve a good relationship, on which you can build a really obedient dog, the owner needs to represent initially the source of food and comfort, training and correction in replacement of the dam. You should not desert the puppy when it most needs your support. Some people advocate putting a pup to bed with ticking alarm clocks, and hot water bottles, but Boxers are too clever to be taken in like that; warm people are best for them.

If you keep the pup with you in this early stage, you are also best placed to take it out to the garden when it stirs at first light, so there is no break at all in training. Only when the pup knows your home thoroughly, understands the word 'No!' and is also confident when left for a short while, is it time to start him sleeping downstairs. By this time, the puppy will take correction in a more constructive manner, having learnt to trust your innate goodness and sense of fair play. Do not have the puppy *on* your bed, just near enough to stretch a hand out to soothe it is quite sufficient.

Since Boxers have such difficulty in keeping their own company, it is wise to start training them to do so at once, but do it when the task is most likely to succeed; when the pup is full of food and tired; after the mid-day meal is a good time. From the first day, leave the pup for ten to fifteen minutes while you go into another room, but try to be back by the time the pup wakes, so that it does not go into a panic. Gradually lengthen the time, until the pup can do an hour or so, but do not take this as a signal that you can be away that length of time every day, or early in the day. A lot of people think they can work in the mornings and leave the Boxer content, but this is the worst time, when they are most awake, and active and need company.

We find that when Boxers have done damage in the house, it is usually when there have been callers in the owner's absence. The dog could not get to them, so in frustration it will bite the woodwork, tear the glass cloth, or rip up the mat. Frustration plays a big part in Boxer lives. It is not always possible to prevent it, but wise to try to eliminate the reaction as far as you can. When you leave the puppy, always lay pads of newspaper near the door, as disturbance brings on the urge to urinate.

Boxers are usually very good in the car, as there is plenty to watch while you are away, but do remember how quickly cars heat up inside, and do not run the risk of cooking your puppy in a tin box. Dogs have died in cars in only moderately hot weather, and they have also got themselves hung through getting gear levers and door handles through their collars. They really are dependent relatives who need to be thought about and for, all the time.

Lead training is the next accomplishment for your puppy, and it is very important to get it right, for a Boxer which tows its owner about is an abomination, shame-making to be seen with and very tiring too. Again, you start by not letting the errors happen. A rolled leather collar and separate, average length lead are best for training. The choke or check collar so beloved by training groups is for dogs which pull and must be broken of the habit. The great secret of lead training is not be going anywhere when you do it. Encourage the pup along, in the garden, keeping the lead short so that the dog is just at your side.

A Boxer's place is with its owner, but giving no pressure on the lead at all. You encourage your pup with a cheerful voice, to get it moving, but if it gets ahead of you, turn and go the other way, so that the pup has to come alongside you again. A folded lead or rolled newspaper waved just ahead of the nose, saying, 'Get back', is a help. The best time for this practice is when the pup is a little tired, and perhaps about five minutes before it is fed. Use your superior knowledge to give the lesson at the time it is most likely to be successful, and at the end, reward with a little titbit and lots of praise. Two or three minutes of lead training every day will get the message home. Make getting out the lead a sign of great joy, but if training is not getting through, take the lead off without comment and give up for that day. Never let the dog enjoy making a fool of you.

Children are always very anxious to take a new puppy out into the street, but there are several reasons against it. One is that they may allow the pup to pull, and so inculcate the idea that this is a thing that can be done. Then you will

Long leather lead for training with either a rolled leather collar or a
check chain. The check chain must be put on correctly

have to un-teach that idea which is harder than teaching something useful. The other is that Boxers do not really need much formalised exercise until they are over six months old, as they should not be allowed to put too much strain on developing joints. Ideally, one would say no road walking until over six months old, but by then the dog is perhaps shy for want of familiarisation with noises and crowds. So do the minimum of road walking to achieve a nice balance but do not go in for endurance tests until the dog is fully mature.

Free running exercise is quite a different matter from pounding the pavements, and the dog should be allowed to play while it is willing to do so. Boxers run in circles, very fast for a few minutes. Their favourite play is to run straight at their owners, and you have to trust that they will put their brakes on, or divert slightly, before they hit you. If you feel nervous when a Boxer is running full speed, hang on to a tree, or stand with your back to the wall. They do have this disconcerting habit of launching themselves without thought for where they land, and Boxer play, particularly in the males and with a person they judge can stand up to it, is very rough indeed.

For walking in a busy town, use a very short lead for the adult dog, so that you have full control in case of a startling noise. Boxers react very suddenly to loud noises, as a guard dog should. They also show great objection to someone walking close behind them, and you may have to keep a very firm hold on your dog in these circumstances.

Boxers vary very much in their need for correction. A soft bitch will never need more than a grumbling word, some even show contrition before you know what it is they have done. A strong-willed male, on the other hand, will often try defying its owner, seeing how far it can go, a mood which seems to come over them at about twelve to eighteen months old, and may require a confrontation and a token 'good hiding' just to make sure who is the more powerful. Punishment should never be administered by a human in a temper; that is ugly; but sometimes the really tough dog will need to be shown superior physical strength before he settles into his place.

Any dog caught in flagrant disobedience reacts well to the sharp slap, especially if it is totally unexpected, but it must be on the instant of disobedience, not for something committed hours before, as the dog cannot associate past deeds with your present actions. They are also very impressed by magic . . . like a stone hurled at the wall behind them, or a voice shouting from an upstairs window when they thought they were unobserved. If your puppy is scratching at a door, bang on the other side, just where its nose would be . . . that carries a lot of impact.

The dog which will not come back to you when called is a great exasperator, and a danger to itself and others. Stop the habit before it starts, by often calling the dog to you, long before you mean to go home. Give a titbit, or better still, praise and caresses, making coming to you always a pleasure. Dogs which will not come because they are interested in something else, will often respond if you turn and walk away. Boxers are very disconcerted if they think they may lose their owner.

The dog that tries to beat you time and time again, especially the one that makes you furious by coming nearly to arm's length and then dodging, must

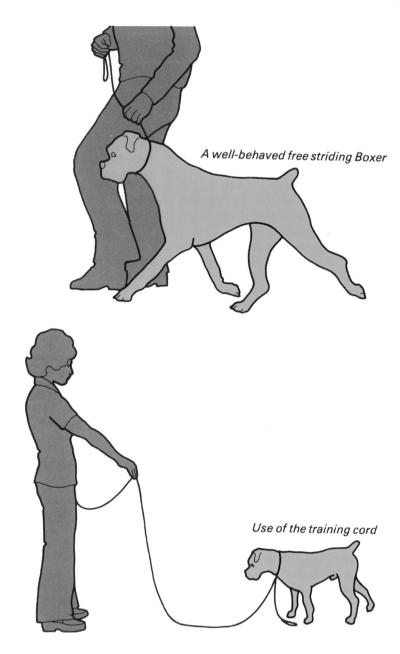

A well-behaved free striding Boxer

Use of the training cord

*Teach the 'sit' by
gently pushing down
the hindquarters*

have another ruse played on it. When you attach the lead to the collar, attach also a six foot length of cord. You can either let the dog go free, and then tread on, or grab the cord when it is teasing you, or you can keep hold of the cord, gradually hauling the dog in as you call it, then giving the reward.

Getting the dog to sit on command is a great help. Teach the 'sit' by gently pushing down the hindquarters, saying the word. Just before you put the feeding bowl down is a good time to 'sit'. If you can get the 'sit' and 'down' absolutely automatic, these commands may be invaluable in emergency in keeping your dog out of trouble. More dogs have been run over by their owners calling to them to come, than if the dog had taken its own line, which is usually to fear traffic. These little episodes of training, practised in odd moments, not only make for an obedient and trouble-free dog, they also induce you to spend time with the animal, giving it your exclusive attention, so it pays double dividends.

There are evening training classes in almost every town in Britain. The veterinary surgeon can probably give details. The atmosphere in these classes varies tremendously. Some concentrate on very high standard competitive work, demanding very accurate 'sits' and immaculate retrieves. We must admit that the Boxer is not a natural for this type of work at which the Alsatian and Border Collie excel. So it is disheartening to go to this type of class, where often the Boxer will not be very welcome, as its clownish sense of humour upsets the more dedicated obedience dogs.

Some clubs also have a puppy class, which is excellent. No formal training is taught, but the puppies are allowed to socialise, and to be handled by other people, a kind of nursery school atmosphere which is enjoyed by pups and owners alike. It is best to get the Boxer to this type of class just as soon as the inoculation course is over, as they soon become rather too large to be acceptable to play with small breed puppies . . . or the owners may think so, anyway.

I hope you may never need to know about a lost Boxer, but it can happen that your dog mislays you, as Tigger did recently when he was thrown through the windscreen of the car. He should not have been sitting on the front seat, of course. One's instinct is to search and scour the country over miles . . . or between the place the dog was last seen and its home, but in most of the 'lost' cases I have known, the dog is found again very close to where it was lost, returning to the place where it last saw its owner. Do not despair if you return to the place and do not see the dog. It is quite likely to be watching you from some little way off, unless it has been temporarily diverted by well meaning people trying to catch it.

The thing to do, and we have proved it, is to sit down quietly, in a field or hedgerow and wait, and wait. If you have to go away leave a coat or some largish article with your own scent. Dogs lost on country walks will return to their car, or to where the car was, but Boxers are not so easy to lose, so it may never occur.

You will also want to notify the police, in case the dog has been taken into someone's home, sometimes not the kindest thing to do, especially if the home is in another county, for liaison by police forces on dogs is not given great priority. You should notify separately all the police forces in surrounding county towns, and do describe the large brown dog. Even now it is not enough to say a Boxer. Not all policemen are dedicated dog men, and some confuse a Boxer with a Bulldog. You might ring up to enquire for your Boxer, and they will not think to tell you they have a 'Mastiff' in the kennels, so don't take anything for granted when making your enquiries.

Toilet and care

Boxers seldom need baths, and total immersion of them is impractical anyway, so a good sponge down, with several buckets of rinsing water, is the best way. A good dog shampoo should be used, never detergent, but if the coat is scurfy, a human dandruff remover is useful. A dampened chamois leather will get rid of surface dust from the coat, and the white bits look very glamorous if sponged over, but the gleaming coat shine really comes from inside, with superlative health and correct nourishment.

A dull and scurfy coat may be improved by adding a little vegetable oil to the food, if the puppy can take it without upset. The nails of puppies need to be clipped about once weekly, with ordinary nail scissors. Older dogs should keep their nails short by a normal amount of walking on pavements or running on beaches, except for the very old dog, which always has an accelerated growth of nail to be taken off by the vet.

Boxers do not usually harbour fleas. They do not seem to have a chemical attraction for them as some breeds do. If you find the flea tracks, the black dots of their excreta, usually just above the dog's tail, you turn the dog over quickly. You may find a flea scampering away in the inguinal area. Fleas may be combed out with a very fine toothed comb, and dunked into methylated spirit. The best anti-parasitic powders are only obtainable from veterinary surgeons

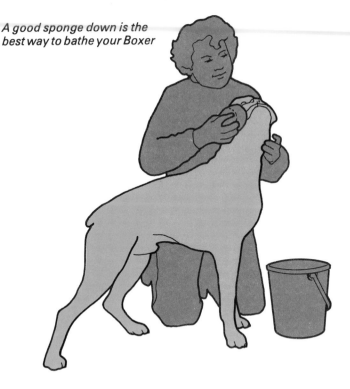

A good sponge down is the best way to bathe your Boxer

in Britain; a good one is well worth getting, as quite a little does an effective job. Remember to attend to beds and carpets too, and also to any cats in the household, with a powder specially formulated for cats. Boxers frequently pick up fleas from hedgehogs in the garden, and as their skins are so sensitive, they may produce an allergy to fleabite which is much more difficult to get rid of than the actual fleas.

Ears need to be kept clean. They should be gently wiped out with a little benzl benzoate mixed with surgical spirit. It is dangerous to probe further than you can see, and cotton wool on sticks should not be used. Itching ears need veterinary attention, as it is all too easy for ear mites to colonise the natural wax, and to give rise to a chronic smelly ear which costs a lot of money to cure. Many household cats carry ear mites which will infect the dog, so they will need treatment as well. Smelly ears make the dog repulsive, so do bad teeth and warts on the gums. It is such a pity to have to reject the dog's affection because it is unpleasant to be near, for the veterinary surgeon can help all these conditions.

Eyes sometimes get full of dust or sand, and look reddened and sore. An ordinary saline eye wash, in use for humans, will clear the eye of this foreign matter, and should be used as a matter of course on seaside holidays.

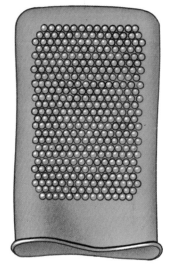

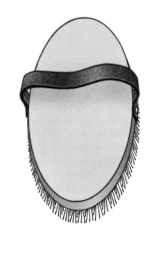

Dandy brush

Grooming glove

Trimming scissors

Fine toothed comb

Boxers do not tolerate the heat especially well, so it is best not to exercise them in the hottest part of the day, and if a journey must be undertaken in great heat, carry some ice with you. It will be very welcome, both to lick and also to have rubbed on the nose, around the stop, and on the head of an over-heated dog. Shade of some sort should be provided on beaches, and a bottle of fresh water must always be carried. Sea water makes dogs sick, and mild salt poisoning will also induce frequent urination.

It is wise to rinse the coat in fresh water after a swim in the sea. Otherwise, a good brush with a stiff dandy brush, about once a week keeps Boxer coats looking trim. When hair is being shed, it is best to get as much out as possible. A rubber glove, drawn down the coat will bring out a surprising amount, otherwise there are special ridged grooming mitts which can be bought.

The ends of docked tails sometimes become sore, causing irritation and making the dog turn in circles to nibble it. A re-docking may be the only answer.

A 'tiger' brindle

Exhibiting and show training

If you have a goodlooking Boxer, it will not be long before someone will tell you that you ought to show it, and it is surprising how many owners think this puts an obligation upon them. In fact, dog showing involves a very great commitment, for it is no use to go once, or even occasionally. It is a hobby which will take up most of your weekends and some weekdays as well. In order to be eligible for competition, the dog must be registered in the correct division at the Kennel Club, and transferred into your ownership. If a spayed bitch, it must already have had a litter which is registered at the Kennel Club. A castrated male cannot be exhibited at all.

It is courteous to visit the breeder before beginning on the show circuit, as many dogs bought purely as companions are entered in shows, perhaps do not do well, and bring adverse criticism on the breeder. So it is as well to take advice about the suitability of the dog from one who knows what the competition is like.

It will be almost essential to go to ringcraft training at your local canine society. This is entirely different from obedience or social training, in that the dog is taught to pose, to be examined by a 'judge' and you are taught to lose your nerves and help your dog make the best of itself. Now that it is becoming increasingly usual to employ professional handlers in the Boxer ring, it is difficult for the novice to do well, as Boxers are not the easiest dogs to show. The Open Show with breed classes is probably your best choice for starting; you will find these advertised in the weekly dog papers; entries are made four to six weeks ahead of the show date.

Show preparation is minimal in the Boxer. Any excess of hair on the edges of the thighs and front legs should be removed, and the facial whiskers cut off with scissors . . . it doesn't hurt! Toenails should be short, and each one polished with vaseline, if you have the patience. The coat will have had all dead hair removed, well brushed and sprayed with a little mink oil coat dressing before being polished with a velvet pad. White areas are lightly damped and then rubbed with chalk, which is brushed out. Remove all chalk after the show as it can destroy the hair if left in. See that the eyes are clean, and the ears.

Boxers are shown on a fine nylon slip lead, never a leather collar which will obscure the rise of the neck. It is usual to take into the ring some squeaky toy, or an attractive titbit, perhaps dried liver or cheese, in order to attract the dog and make it look alert when the judge's eye is on it.

The continental habit of having outsiders around the edge of the ring to attract the dog is very much frowned on in Britain.

A conventional show pose with tail and chin supported

Health

Vets

Before you buy your puppy it is prudent to make contact with a veterinary surgeon, one specialising in small animal work. In Britain try to find a member of the British Small Animal Veterinary Association, as vets who deal almost entirely with farm livestock, or horses, are not so likely to have the current knowledge, or the equipment for dog emergencies. It is also important that you find a vet whose personality suits yours, someone you can talk to, and, above all, trust. It is useful if the vet of your choice feels some affinity with Boxers too, for vets are only people with white coats on. They have their prejudices, and sometimes their fears, and they don't do their best work if they have an innate dislike of the breed they are handling.

In America, veterinarians never make house calls. In Britain some will, and some will not, so if this factor is likely to be of importance, make enquiry first. If you are without transport, it can be difficult to find someone who will happily drive a vomiting, or bleeding Boxer to surgery. Find out about the surgery hours, whether they will fit with your lifestyle; and also what facilities the surgery has, for anaesthetics, X-ray, or perhaps cryosurgery, a 'cold finger' technique specially suitable for Boxer skin tumours or warts on the gums.

Some veterinary practices are designated as 'hospitals' in Britain and this indicates that they have in-patient facilities for dogs and cats. Do not be overawed about asking questions, for you will be paying the bill, for treatment, drugs, surgery and residential care. It is usual for vets to dispense their own drugs in Britain and USA, except for products which have a very short shelf life. In Europe drugs are more frequently obtained from chemists, and there is some indication that as members of the EEC, this may become the rule in Britain too.

Veterinary treatment always seems expensive in Britain, though in USA, where people are accustomed to paying for their own health problems, veterinary bills are more easily tolerated. There is no point in 'shopping around.' There is usually an agreement between practices on fees, but you can save yourself a lot of money by good observation of your dog, and careful presentation of the history of an illness, cutting down the need for exploratory treatments.

In America vets are addressed as Doctor; in Britain Doctors and Professors denote that a post graduate degree has been earned, and most vets of this rank are working in universities and research establishments.

The best way to find your vet is by recommendation from another dog owner, or perhaps the breeder of your puppy. Unfortunately vets are judged by successes, not just for trying, so make your enquiries fairly wide. If you find the vet of your first choice is not the man you can get on with, you can always change, but between illnesses only. To go somewhere else while a condition is being treated is not only discourteous and unethical, it may also do the dog a disservice, if you hide what drugs or treatments have already been given. In cases of long-standing illness, it is wise to ask for a second opinion, which should be from someone not in the same practice, and should be arranged for you without question. Such cases are frequently referred to veterinary schools for evaluation, especially when it is known a study on a particular disease is in progress.

Boxer in illness

The veterinary surgeon is not only the dog's doctor, but also dentist, X-ray technician, gynaecologist, brain specialist, and perhaps ambulance service as well. He is an expert at diagnosis and treatment, but only you know your dog well enough to say when he needs treatment. Only you can learn to be discriminating about when you must call the vet immediately, when you must go tomorrow if there is no improvement, and when you can afford to take time to allow nature's own healing to operate. Many conditions do get better with home care, especially the slight bumps, bruises and accidents which happen, provided the dog is in superb health. The young, the elderly, and those debilitated by other disorders will need the help of modern drugs to combat many incidents which the healthy dog will take in its stride, and overcome with simple home care remedies of the kind you would apply to children. If you regard your Boxer in this aspect as you would a child of about six years, you will not go far wrong.

Sometimes, going to the vet too early can be a waste of time and money on both sides, for though you have a suspicion that something is amiss, the only advice that can be given is to wait and see what develops. So you have to be vigilant and watch your dog's behaviour, and take its temperature, as this is a great indicator of infection developing. Use a stubby ended thermometer, obtainable from any chemist, and kept exclusively for the dog. The dog's temperature should be 101.5°F (38.6°C) in the rectum. With the Boxer, there is no need to use vaseline on the thermometer, which should be inserted about 1½in. (3cm.) into the rectum, and held there for one and a half minutes, then wiped with a tissue and read. Take temperatures with the dog standing, and someone else to hold the front end steady, but if you prefer and feel more control, have the dog lying on its side. Temperatures can be reported to the veterinary surgery over the telephone, together with other symptoms; this will help the vet to advise about the necessity of bringing the dog to the surgery.

As the Boxer is normally so exuberant, and such a creature of habit, it is quite easy to see when an adult is unwell, when you are familiar with its normal behaviour pattern. When Blossom refuses food, we worry because it *must* be serious. But if Tigger and Naiad say no thank you, we let them wait for a day, confident that when they need food, they will take it.

This differential diagnosis is more difficult in the young puppy, partly because its behaviour pattern is not yet formulated, and also because you have less time available to you to wait for a natural cure, as little puppies go downhill very quickly in infections, and also with dehydration in cases of diarrhoea. The latter is the most frequent worry in puppies, possibly because all changes of feeding are of an experimental nature in puppies, and also through their own wicked ways of eating things which should never be eaten; and of course, they are liable to more infections of a local nature when they move from the environment of their first home.

A prostrated, vomiting, diarrhoeaic puppy, with or without blood in the faeces, needs the vet at once. A cheerful, playing puppy having loose motions can afford to wait twelve hours to see what a light diet, rest, warmth, and care will do.

Never give any Boxer who is off-colour any exercise, or even vigorous play. The dog's natural remedy is to seek peace, warmth and quiet, and to fast.

In diarrhoea it is important to offer cooled boiled water, perhaps containing glucose (1 tablespoonful per ½pt. (¼l.) as often as the puppy will take it, unless it is obvious that drinking to excess brings on vomiting, in which case, having reported this symptom to the vet, the water must be offered in controlled small amounts pending further advice. The dog can live without food for quite some time, but water is an essential to life.

Unless on vet's advice, diarrhoea should not be 'dried up' with commercial remedies, as it may be important for the puppy's body to rid itself of poisonous matter.

One worry to owners that is not really an illness is the puppy's distasteful habit of re-consuming its own excreta, a habit which rightly disgusts the owner, but does not seem bad to an animal. If it finds an edible substance, down it goes! Some tinned meats, processed to be appealing to both dog and the owner, sometimes pass too quickly through the intestine, before all useful substances are absorbed, and so the excreta contains something attractive and edible.

A change to plainer and more totally digested diets usually breaks the habit, and picking up and disposing of the excreta quickly will prevent it happening, and a little slap if caught in the act of eating will show that this is something of which the owner does not approve.

Puppies make many experiments in eating and you will find stones, coal, wood and plants go down. If you catch the puppy swallowing stones, or in the act of taking some poison, the quicker you get to the vet, the better the outlook will be.

Ears are carried at all angles when the pup is cutting its second teeth, from four to eight months. There is nothing you or the vet can do to make them come right, except wait hopefully. The head held to one side, one ear permanently lower than the other, indicates some pain in the facial region which may be teeth, eyes or ears. An adult can be given an aspirin, and wait a day or two, according to general health, to see if it was caused by one of the many bangs a Boxer inflicts upon itself. If you play this waiting game with any symptom, do make a note when you first saw it, as this may be of great help if you seek veterinary advice in the end.

Eyes with a purulent discharge may indicate an infection, or misplaced eyelids, or eyelashes rubbing on the cornea, (ectropion, entropion, and distichiasis are the correct names), a not uncommon affliction on that rather folded-up Boxer face. Sometimes this condition will improve when the face is finally formed at eighteen months to two years, or your veterinary surgeon may consent to operate to relieve suffering, although this operation is known as 'cosmetic' and will not be performed to improve a Boxer for showing, and the afflicted animal should not be used for breeding, or the condition will be perpetuated.

A vet will identify the eye condition for you with special diagnostic tools. A blue film suddenly appearing over the eye may be a corneal ulcer, caused by injury to the surface of the eye. A vet can help with special eye drops, but do be **wary of using one kind of eye medication on a subsequent condition; you** could do harm and hinder healing. You can always have a word on the telephone with the vet. They prefer to feel you consult them, and if you are able to impress with your commonsense, and willingness to seek advice when it is needed, you will find that you are allowed some remedies to use at your

discretion, for vets understand just how the Boxer gets itself into trouble.

Wet noses do not count for anything. Some dogs have very wet black blobs with a large amount of clear fluid, others have dry noses, especially when they have been tucked down in warm places. A thick catarrhal discharge is always a cause for professional advice.

It will be the lucky Boxer puppy which gets through its first summer without having nettlerash (urticaria), when great wheals come up all over the body suddenly, and look so alarming. They are caused by an allergy, perhaps actually to nettles or some other plant, perhaps to insect or flea bites. If the face and tongue are badly involved, it will be best to contact the vet, as the Boxer cannot tolerate any swelling in that region. Otherwise, rest and quiet will see the wheals going down quite soon, helped by an anti-histamine tablet which you can buy off prescription, but which also has a tranquillising effect. If urticaria happens often, you must make some observation of the related conditions, and go to the vet armed with the history, otherwise you start, expensively, from scratch.

Wasp and bee stings are also dangerous in the mouth, throat and nose, anywhere there is natural congestion which may obstruct breathing. Otherwise, bathing with bicarbonate of soda, or a paste of that substance rubbed on, will give relief. Stings should be pulled out if they can be seen. The Boxer makes a great fuss of licking any injury like this, so you must investigate the spot, and it will be considerably calmed by the fact that you have looked at it. Dogs are very childlike in this way.

Because of reckless play, Boxers get injured. Badly bleeding wounds should be covered by a large pad, bandaged on, and taken to the vet for suturing. A deep punctured wound, made by a tooth, or a piece of wire, looks less alarming, but may by more dangerous, as it penetrates into deep tissue. Vet treatment is essential. Torniquets should not be applied except by those with nursing training.

Torn ears bleed an awful lot, and if shaken, make a great deal of mess. They may be bandaged back to the head, and held there by an ingenious cap made from the elastic net bandage sold for human injuries.

Sore throats are indicated by stretching the throat constantly towards the ceiling. If caused by barking, sand or dust, a day's rest and some honey to lick will help, but if the temperature is also raised, you need a vet's help.

A peculiar kind of cough that sounds like a fish bone in the throat may indicate a case of kennel cough, an epidemic disease which is picked up by droplet wherever dogs meet when there is an outbreak. It seems to move around the country frequently in the summer when dogs are gathered together in boarding kennels. Get telephone advice on this one, do not spread it further by taking the dog into surgery unless you are asked to.

Boxers sometimes get hot liquids spilt on their backs and at least, in Boxers, you can see the damage. Cool at once with cold water, and ask for advice.

Itching and scratching come from many causes; coat change, fleas, or lice are the easiest to sort out. Boxer claws used with Boxer energy soon make the skin raw, and ready for a secondary infection to take hold, so do not let scratching go on long.

First aid dressing for a badly cut foot prior to professional attention

An excessive thirst, and almost uncontrollable amounts of urine are danger signals, so is frequent urination in the bitch, except near oestrus when they may do some form of 'marking' in the manner of the dog. Try to get a urine sample to take to the vet. Collect it in an old long-handled frying pan.

An arched back, indicating abdominal pain, also needs quick advice and a comprehensive history of eating patterns, and also anything torn up, swallowed, or even anything missing may help the vet.

Boxers sometimes faint, under stress or in hot weather, due to the congestion in the blood vessels and nerves of the back of the throat. Treat as for human faint, with an ice pack, and ice to lick, and if it happens frequently, get veterinary advice.

The young dog which often sits to rest when out for a normal length walk, also needs looking at as there is some tendency to heart disease, and some hip dysplasia in the breed, although very few dogs have enough hip disfunction to show clinical lameness. Hip Dysplasia, a malformation of the joint between pelvis and the head of the femur, is usually discovered on X-ray for some other condition, and should not alarm the average owner too much, as the dog will more than likely not show any effects. HD is thought to be a hereditary condition aggravated by over weight and over excercise in the puppy stage.

As in other large breeds, there is epilepsy in some Boxer strains, though this is usually only detectable around two years old. The epileptic animal is quite easy to live with. Drugs may be prescribed to control the condition, or may not be necessary at all if the fits are mild or infrequent. The epileptic dog always has the fits when it is bored or in its sleep, *never* when it is playing, or at exercise or in the show ring. Getting excited does not bring on a fit, and the Boxer does not attack people when having one. Protect the dog from a dangerous situation while in the fit, and leave it in calm dark and quiet surroundings to recover. Tell the veterinary surgeon afterwards. The same advice applies to a heart attack, which looks roughly the same but usually without the shaking syndrome. After a heart attack or 'stroke' the dog may be very disorientated or bewildered about its surroundings. Give lots of reassurance, but do not let it go up and down the stairs, looking for it does not know quite what, as old Poppet was inclined to do after one of her 'turns'. Rest, covered with a blanket, is essential.

Discharges from the vulva of the bitch in between seasons, or just after a season should have finished, warrants investigation, as the wide open vulva of the Boxer bitch is prone to infection. A sad and sorry girl, drinking large amounts of water, may also have a uterine infection which is worse because it is not discharging. A useful clue is that male dogs find these conditions interesting by scent, so if your bitch continues to attract dogs, have her checked.

Lumps in the mammary glands should be removed as soon as possible, as mammary tumours are quite common in the breed and there is a fair chance that they may be malignant and may spread to the lungs, with inevitably fatal results. Malignancy can only be diagnosed under the microscope after the tumour is removed, and bears no relationship to whether the tumour is increasing visibly or not. Research work done by the Animal Health Trust Small Animal Centre, in England, has greatly improved the outlook on mammary tumours, so do have them taken off while they are small.

Boxer skin is particularly prone to small wart-like growths which come up with no apparent cause, though possibly they are of viral origin. If they raise well above the coat surface, and are inclined to bleed, they should be removed by the vet. They seldom give trouble, although hair may not grow again on the place.

Possibly the worst of all emergencies is stomach torsion and bloat, a condition occuring most of all in larger breeds than the Boxer, but just occasionally in this breed as an extension of its habitual 'rumbling tum' and nervous indigestion. The overfilled stomach tends to twist on itself, blocking the exit, and causing acute pain, the only time your Boxer will scream in agony. This is an acute emergency when minutes count in getting to the vet. No home treatment can help.

To guard against bloat and torsion we always soak biscuit, and never give a heavy dry meal on which the dog may drink a big quantity of water. Some people restrict water for an hour or two after meals. We do not exercise the dogs after feeding either, and in dogs with a tendency to bloating, feed twice a day in smaller amounts. Bloat frequently occurs at night, and is invariably fatal in the dog shut away in a kennel unobserved. A true case of bloat is easily visible. The stomach swells to alarming proportions while you watch. A minor case can be very painful, so do not hesitate in finding a vet, any vet, at once. This is no time for professional courtesies if you are out of touch with your regular surgery.

The natural exuberance of the Boxer is such a feature of the breed, that when this diminishes at all, it is a good indication that something is amiss. More sluggish breeds hide illness more easily, a coated breed has more camouflage. Depression in the Boxer usually means illness, but it can mean unjust punishment has been given, which the Boxer feels keenly. Even harsh words or shouting will upset a soft-hearted Boxer bitch and they will also become subdued when one of the family goes away, and sometimes, if they are taken away from their familiar surroundings. In general, the adult Boxer keeps in very good health, only seeing the vet for the annual boosters of preventative vaccinations, and possibly treatments for the accidents which being a bouncy Boxer may bring.

The sick or elderly Boxer can benefit from the wearing of a coat tailored to protect the chest

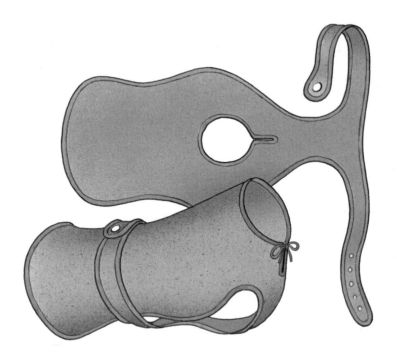

The old Boxer

Boxers in common with other short-faced breeds are not among the longest lived dogs; anything over ten years is a bonus, though twelve is not uncommon. Hair colour fades early; Naiad has the first greying on her muzzle at four; Poppet's mask is almost entirely grey now, and her coat colour has faded too. In the brindles, the stripes may blur and run together, giving a patchy effect, probably due to hormonal imbalance.

Improvement in veterinary knowledge and increased awareness in the owner all combine to make our dogs today live a lot longer than their earlier forbears.

It is important that Boxers over six years old should have six-monthly check-ups by the vet, and that urinalysis is particularly included, so that function of the internal organs may be monitored, and treatment started before damage to kidneys etc. has gone too far to be improved.

As in the human, eyesight and hearing begin to fail in the elderly, and the sense of smell is also diminished.

The muscle in the hindlegs is inclined to atrophy with age, making the elderly dog a little tottery, but with veterinary help so much of life with the owner can still be enjoyed, if taken at a slower pace. The vet can prescribe painkillers for rheumatism, and tablets to stimulate heart action, or drugs to relieve incontinence, and other distressing symptoms.

Removal of decayed teeth and the papillomas which grow inside the mouth can give a renewed interest in eating with considerable impact on the general metabolism and well being.

Nails tend to become overgrown in old age and clipping by the vet will make walking more comfortable, so adding to the elderly dog's scope and interest.

Digestion may be helped by specially prescribed diets, or the normal food can be broken down into two or three meals each day to aid digestion. In acute phases, a liquid protein food as used for human invalids, will give sustenance when appetite is poor.

All owners who have enjoyed the company of their Boxer right into old age will wish that one day it would lie down in its basket and die in its sleep. Unfortunately, such mercy is very seldom granted, and it is most often necessary to take a deliberate decision when life no longer holds any enjoyment for the dog. In the hands of a competent veterinary surgeon euthanasia by means of the injection of an overdose of anaesthetic into the dog's front leg should hold no terror for owner or the dog. It is sad, but not ugly. The owner should support the dog, perhaps helping the vet by raising a vein, while the fluid is injected, and the animal will collapse gently within sixty seconds. A premedication of tranquillising pills may be given if the vet thinks it necessary. Euthanasia by cheaper methods, for example electrocution cabinets, are not the method of choice for the pet dog. If the dog is extremely old and ill, and circulation is poor, the injection may have to be made directly into the heart, when there will be a little more reaction, but it is painless to the dog. It is best, especially for the old dog, if the vet will come to the home to do this last service.

It is, I think, the owner's duty to be present at the end. I find it inconceivable that, in order to escape sadness, a dog can be handed over to surgery staff to feel bewilderment and desertion in its last moments. Veterinary surgeons who have problems inter-relating to their clients may try to prevent the owner being present, in order to save themselves the strain of coping with emotion. If you have doubts about your vet's attitude, discuss the matter first and go elsewhere if you are not suited. The dog matters most at this time.

The veterinary surgeon is not an undertaker, and has no obligation to dispose of bodies, especially if they are not his patients, but most make some provision for the animals of their clients. There are also private crematoria for animals, giving a service at variable expense according to the degree of approximation to a human cremation that is required. Your veterinary surgeon can tell you what facilities there are available for the disposal of animal carcases in your local area.

At the time of parting with a well-loved friend it may seem unlikely that you will ever risk going through such unhappiness again, but there will come a time when the house seems too immaculate, the hearth too empty, and you will miss so much the sound of warm snores in the night. Once a Boxer owner, always a Boxer owner, and I predict that you will find another puppy which appeals to you, and you will go through the exciting Boxer saga all over again.

Peaceful old age

Addresses:

Boxerama Magazine, Numbers 1-8
The Editor, *Boxerama,*
The Sun Inn, Corfton, nr. Craven Arms, Salop, England.

Dog World, 32 New Street, Ashford, Kent, England.

Our Dogs, Oxford Road Station Approach, Manchester, England.

The Kennel Club, 1/4 Clarges Street, London W.1. England.

The American Kennel Club, and magazine *Pure Bred Dogs,*
51 Madison Avenue, New York, N.Y.10010, USA.

American Boxer Club, c/o Carl A. Wood, Woodcrest, Rappahannock Drive, P.O.
Box 668, White Stone, VA 22578.

The British Boxer Club, c/o Mrs. J. Clayton, Durnfield Farm, Tintinhull, Nr.
Yeovil, Somerset.

Boxer Rescue Service: Mr. Les Crawley, Brighton 505770; Mr. H. Adams,
Brighton 778320.

The Dog Directory, Binfield Park, Bracknell, Berks.

Puppy Enquiries: Dog Breeder Associates, c/o Mrs. S. Blumire, 1 Abbey Road,
Bourne End, Bucks. Tel: Bourne End, 20943.

London and Home Counties Boxer Club,
c/o Mrs. I.P. Wilsdow, Hedgerows,
East Hanningfield, Chelmsford, Essex GM3 5AH.

Books:

John F. Gordon. *All About the Boxer.* Pelham Books.

M. Fairbrother and Peggy Thompson. *Boxer Blarney.* Privately published,
obtainable from *Dog World,* England.

Friederun Stockmann. *My Life with Boxers.* Now out of print. A few copies
available, enquire The Pheasantry, East Dean, Chichester, Sussex.

Elizabeth Somerfield. *The Popular Boxer.* Popular Dogs.

Index